MICHAEL ANTHONY

The Year in San Fernando

Introduction by
Paul Edwards
& Kenneth Ramchand

H·E·B

HEINEMANN EDUCATIONAL BOOKS

IN ASSOCIATION WITH
ANDRE DEUTSCH

Heinemann Education Books Ltd
22 Bedford Square, London WC1B 3HH
EDINBURGH MELBOURNE AUCKLAND KINGSTON
HONG KONG SINGAPORE KUALA LUMPUR NEW DELHI
IBADAN NAIROBI
Heinemann Educational Books Inc
70 Court Street, Portsmouth, New Hampshire 03801, USA

ISBN 0 435 98031 9

First published in Caribbean Writers Series 1970
Reprinted 1971, 1972
Reset 1976
Reprinted 1976, 1978, 1979, 1983, 1985 (twice)

To
Jennifer, and Keith,
and Yvette

This edition has been completely reset and page numbers
do not now correspond with earlier editions

Printed in Great Britain by
Richard Clay (The Chaucer Press) Ltd,
Bungay, Suffolk

This book is to be returned on or before
the last date stamped below.

CARIBBEAN WRITERS SERIES

CARIBBEAN WRITERS SERIES

ne Year an Fernando

INTRODUCTION

Paul Edwards and Kenneth Ramchand

Michael Anthony's novel records one year in the life of a twelve-year-old boy who leaves his native village Mayaro in Trinidad, for the city, to go to school and work as a servant-companion in the house of an old lady, Mrs Chandles. The experiences of Francis in the novel are based upon a year Michael Anthony himself spent in San Fernando from after Christmas 1943 to just before Christmas 1944, when he was twelve years old. The novel was written in England in the late 1950s and early 1960s, but the author neither imposes adult ways of seeing life on his adolescent narrator, nor allows the older man he himself has become to break into the narrative; from start to finish the experiencing consciousness of the novel is that of the boy, Francis. It is a source of the novel's irony that people and places can be seen objectively through the boy's observing eyes and subjectively in terms of his responses to them, as in this passage where the reader is unlikely to feel the same awe for Mr Chandles as Francis does:

> We had heard only very little about Mr Chandles. The little we had heard were whispers and we didn't gather much, but we saw him sometimes leaning over the banister of the Forestry Office, and indeed he was as aristocratic as they said he was. He looked tidy and elegant and he always wore jacket and tie, unusual under the blazing sun. These things confirmed that he was well off, and his manner and bearing, and the condescending look he gave everything about him, made us feel that he had gained high honours in life. (p. 1)

But it would be wrong to think of this as a work in which the boy's voice is being used either ironically or directly in the interests of satirical social comment. This aspect of the novel is intermittent and unobtrusive, never getting in the way of the reader's illusion of living through the boy's consciousness. One might compare this with Austin Clarke's *Amongst Thistles and Thornes* (1965), where the narrating child is the nine-year-old Milton Sobers. In the quotation below, the scene is a classroom in the colony; it is a state occasion, and the children are singing 'Rule Britannia'. The boy Milton is made to reflect:

> ... the headmaster was soaked in glee. And I imagined all the glories of Britannia, our Motherland, Britannia so dear to us all, and so free; Britannia who, or what or which, had brought us out of the ships crossing over from the terrible seas from Africa, and had placed us on this island, and had given us such good headmasters, and assistant masters, and such a nice vicar to teach us how to pray to God – and he had come from England; and such nice white people who lived on the island with us, and who gave us jobs watering their gardens and taking out their garbage, most of which we found delicious enough to eat. (p. 12)

The crucial difference between the voices of Francis and Milton Sobers is that Milton's is not really a child's voice at all, the sarcasm being too sustained for a nine-year-old. Milton becomes a vehicle for Austin Clarke's very explicit irony, which he is using to make an equally explicit social protest. The problem is not an uncommon one when the author is working through naïve narrators, and can be found from time to time in, for example, Dickens, when the voice of authorial indignation or satire clearly breaks through that of an 'innocent' figure such as Cissy Jupe or Esther Summerson.

Another West Indian novel of childhood, George Lamming's *In the Castle of my Skin* (1953) achieves a powerful evocation of the boy's world; but Lamming's intention is to suggest the essential outlines of *typical boyhood* in a *generalized West Indian community*, one, moreover, that is growing painfully – like the four boys in the novel – into political self-awareness. Sometimes, indeed, the author's concern to suggest the complex shiftings in the community at large takes precedence over any notion of fidelity to the boys' consciousness. In contrast, *The Year in San Fernando*, which is set in the penultimate year of the Second World War, registers neither that event nor the political stirrings in Trinidad of that period.

Geoffrey Drayton's *Christopher* (1959) resembles *The Year in San Fernando* in at least two respects: it works through the very particular consciousness of an isolated boy; and it does not have an explicit social or political message. But *Christopher* concentrates on a period in the life of a boy which we recognize as crucial, an easily grasped theme defined with ultimate obviousness in the final paragraph. Christopher cannot suppress his desolation during the burial of his nurse, Gip. He tries to leap into the grave but is caught and taken to his anxious mother:

> . . . then as the high wail went up, she held him against her. And her body shook and she did not know if she was weeping for Gip or weeping because he was again the child that Gip had nursed – a child . . . for a few minutes more as he clung to her, he was a child – a few minutes more that were the last of his childhood. (p. 192)

This is the most contrived paragraph in the novel, but what it attempts to underline is a theme – the passing of childhood – which is implicit in Drayton's organization of the work and which allows us to put down the novel satisfied that we know exactly what it is all about. Now in the final paragraph of *The Year in San Fernando* we find Francis on a bus taking him back to Mayaro:

> I closed the window because the rains were almost pouring down now. I sat down cosily and there was a lot of talking inside the bus. It was cosy to sit with the windows closed and the rains pouring and the bus speeding along the wet road. The talking was very cheerful. I remembered the mountain and suddenly I looked back but all the windows were closed because of the rains. The bus roared on, and my mind went on Mrs Chandles, who was dying, and Mr Chandles – so strange of late, and now homeless; and I thought also of Mrs Princet, and I thought of Edwin and that dollar – I thought of all the mixed-up things, of all the funny things, in fact, which made the year at Romaine Street. (p. 137)

Childhood has not 'passed'. The experiencing consciousness of the boy continues to flow, there is nothing apparently definitive, final, no obvious resolution to the tale.

It is not entirely surprising, then, that Anthony's refusal to impose easily identifiable themes, and the absence of a traditional story-line have been misunderstood in the West Indies, where commentators, have complained about the novel's lack of 'form', 'philosophy', and 'significance':

> ... the book is an apparently meaningless chronicle with no foundation in any strong or profound philosophy. It moves along unrelieved and in the end signifies little.

Thus says a reviewer in *Bim*, who continues patronizingly,

> I feel too that there is a brave attempt at profundity somewhere in the conception of the book, but all that comes off the page is a very weak suggestion of an unreal something. If Michael Anthony had wanted to chronicle the profundities latent in a loss of innocence – which would have called for an essentially much more dynamic mind – it would have been more effective in this case, I think to have made a passionate concentrate of what he now offers us. Seventy-five poignant pages, perhaps, might have made a masterpiece.

As in Barbados, so in Jamaica – *The Year in San Fernando*'s freedom from the obvious in plot or social message has made it appear to lack significance. A review in the *Jamaica Gleaner* of a later novel by Michael Anthony, *Green Days by the River*, repeats an earlier judgement:

> Just as we said of *The Year in San Fernando* the author is extremely accurate in portrayal of each incident so that each and every one sounds authentic so that one is forced to ask the question 'so what?' or 'was the story worth telling?'.

We want to argue that, on the contrary, in *The Year in San Fernando* Anthony is practising an art of a subtle and powerful kind. The novel involves us in the feel of a peculiarly 'open' state of consciousness. This 'open' consciousness differs from the 'normal' in that it fuses elements of experience which we usually see as disparate, or indeed as belonging to opposed categories like nostalgia-anticipation, town-country, pure-sordid and so on. In general, the author achieves this effect by a scrupulous adherence to the boy's point of view in a language that appears simple on the surface but which is sensuous and at times symbolic even while sustaining the illusion of adolescent reportage. Before exploring all this in explanatory detail, it is necessary to take note of how Anthony creates a framework of convention within which the 'open' consciousness functions.

Far from displaying a lack of form the novel is remarkable for a nearly classical observance of the unities: one action (what happens to the boy), one place (the town of San Fernando – he leaves Mayaro after the first chapter), and one time (the year). Francis' physical world is clearly defined – the Chandles' house, places at particular distances from the house (the market, the wharf, etc), and persons and objects (the girl Julia and Mt Naparaima) seen on journeys to and from the house. Within this physically framed world, Francis' behaviour is given pattern by a number of routine or repetitive activities which serve as conventions in the world of the novel in much the same way as social conventions do in real life: going to market, sweeping the house, watering the plants and rubbing Mrs Chandles' legs with Sacrool, 'The Indian Sacred Oil'; or looking at the growing cane and the cane fires in the distant fields, sitting still in the hideaway among the concrete pillars of the tall house, listening to sounds – passing traffic, distant music, voices upstairs – and thinking of the things and people in his life.

Since the novel covers a full year in the boy's life, Anthony is able to use a cycle of natural change and progression as a larger reference into which the novel's structural conventions are absorbed. All the novel's repetitive activities are varied by and become increasingly integrated with the progress of the changing year. The daily round of the market changes subtly as the fruits of different seasons appear on the stalls; at the end of the dry season Mrs Chandles' legs do not have to be rubbed; and the listening boy's ears pick up the swish-swish of tyres on the wet road announcing the arrival of the rainy season. In the dry season, the cane fires are seen drawing closer and closer from the distant fields as the crop comes to an end; and at the same time the plant watering routine is modified to twice a day and different hours to cope with the aridity and heat. But these repetitive activities are registered primarily in terms of the boy's consciousness, the physical impact on him of the world he is growing into; they are not placed in the novel in a mechanical or rigidly systematic way in order that they might strike the reader as symbolic or thematic.

All the more remarkable then is the following extended passage.

After half a year in San Fernando, Francis receives a visit from his mother. The meeting promises much, but the ingratiating behaviour of Mrs Chandles comes between the boy and his mother, and she leaves again without having made the contact both she and her son wish for. As her bus speeds away, the son begins to realize that his chance of escape is receding too:

I thought of the bus speeding away and I walked slowly back to the house. The pavement along Romaine Street rose very prominently from the road and I was just slightly eased of my sadness and I stepped up on to the pavement then down to the pitch again and I walked right down the street like that. In the little spaces between the houses I could see red flickers. They were 'burning-out' – the estate people were. I stood up to watch the fire whenever I came to a little space, and I could hear the crackle and the way the flames roared in the wind. This was the last of the cane-fires, for the crop was nearly ended. Watching the fires had been a great attraction for me through all these months. They had started from far away in that great expanse of green. Now the fires were blazing out the last patch, near the town. I stood up at the big gap between the school and our house, and the fire I could see here stretched over some distance, and the flame-tongues licked the air, and they reddened a large part of the sky between the houses. Away over the brown open field I could see the dusk coming.

I stood up for a while looking at the cane-fire and at the dusk but my mind was wandering and I was thinking of the speeding bus. I wondered how far was she now. I tried to think of sugar-cane. Tomorrow the cutters would come with their cutlasses, and the field, having been scorched of vermin and needless leaves, would be quickly cut down. The mills at the Usine Ste Madeleine would still be grinding, and the three chimneys would still be puffing smoke, but really, the crop would be over. Tomorrow when I got home from school I would see brown earth where the last patch of green used to be. And perhaps the ploughs would come to this little part soon. I had often seen them working in the parts already cleared. Owen, my friend, who had been to all places, said the ploughs made long mounds and furrows as they went along. He said their work was to turn up the earth and to manure it and then the whole place was left alone until planting time. I did not know about all this. I could not see the mounds from here, nor the manure which the ploughs put on. But I had seen the planting at the beginning of the year, and then what looked like endless green fields, and lately, the fires every night. And with the fires, the three chimneys of the Usine Ste Madeleine had started puffing smoke. For they were grinding the cane. When Owen explained it, it seemed very simple for him. But for me there was always a little mystery about the cane.

I left off looking at the fires and I went home again. The thoughts of the cane had held off the feelings of dejection. Now I felt it coming like a storm. (pp. 65–66)

There is a great deal in these paragraphs: the placing of 'The bus speeding away' and 'walked slowly back' on either side of the co-ordinating conjunction which turns out to be the point of separation, so that the structure of the sentence helps to convey its meaning by its movement; the way in which the boy's up and down movement between road and pavement expresses his agitation yet rhythmically soothes it; how the literal approaching dusk at the end of the first paragraph becomes the metaphorical storm of dejection in the last two sentences in the third paragraph. But there is another feature we want to notice particularly. The fires which catch Francis' eyes and offer temporary distraction from his sense of loss are in fact signs of the end of the cane season: at the beginning of the year he had seen 'what looked like endless green fields'; later, he had seen the start of the firing process; now, the last field is being burnt out. The cane fields become an image of the progression of the boy's year in San Fernando, and the 'mystery' of growth and decay. The boy himself is not conscious of this as symbolic, only as a thing seen,

Felt in the blood and felt along the heart,

in the way symbols are best understood, the way in which we as readers respond to the passage in the novel. At this point we should like to remark on the danger of reading critically in a merely analytic way: any analysis or elucidation we offer is intended as no more than a suggestion about the way the novel might be read, not as the answer to some literary puzzle or test. All the same, it is implicit in the design of this novel that at some points the reader is aware of more than the boy Francis is: and in this passage, the boy's depression is intensified as he turns from the cane fields while the reader, who is both inside and outside the boy's consciousness, recognizes the cycle of natural regeneration of which the boy's harrowing period is a part. We are suggesting then that in an apparently spontaneous way, what might so easily have been exotic information about the planting and harvesting of cane comes to serve an archetypal function in the novel. Francis, *told* by Owen about the ploughing and furrowing and the period of lying fallow, 'did not know about all this'. Yet two paragraphs later when he has arrived in the Chandles' house, so subtly does Anthony's art transform the literal into the symbolic, the furrowing is understood and accepted by the boy as a phase in his particular growth:

> ... My eyes looked out on Celesta Street but it was not the lit-up panes I was seeing now. Dejection swept upon me. Now at this hour I was suffering for the need of home. Now I felt a prisoner in this giddy town. My heart was burning for home. For a moment I felt like crying out, but at the moment of greatest pain my mother's voice came back to me. It was as if she was here and talking. She had said, Stay and take in education, boy. Take it in. That's the main thing.
>
> That was about the last thing she had said to me. I heard it now as plain as ever. (p. 67)

There is a pattern of growth in the novel but it is not a growth which will ever seem complete. When Francis first arrives in the town, with its neon signs flashing, its teeming crowds, and its tall strange buildings, towering high above the streets he is more than bewildered: 'Mr Chandles had said one could get lost here so easily. Already I could see myself getting lost. I could see myself wandering hopelessly about this maze of streets. Listening to him, without considering the words themselves, I had the feeling things would be very mixed up when I went out.' (p. 11) it is a metaphor of the book that Francis' bewilderment, and his process of groping towards an understanding of the town, the Chandles' house, and the people who strike him as mysterious, should appear to the reader as part of a continuous process of coming to learn about life:

> ... we were still approaching the school and I was still looking at the weird empty yard when Mr Chandles spoke.

'You'll have to watch this school,' he said, 'This house here is yours.'

The house just before the school was journey's end. (p. 12)

This kind of growing or becoming in the novel may be illustrated with reference to Francis' mastery of marketing skills. This is a literal process and one that Francis himself can measure, but it is also a metaphoric one through which the reader is made aware of a more open-ended journeying. Francis' initial bewilderment at the market is expressed in terms that remind us of his first responses to the town, both suggesting the perplexity of a sensitive confrontation with life:

> The vastness of this interior bewildered me, and also I was amazed by the great mass of people and by the steady roar of human voices which startled you because you saw no one screaming. The roof was all slate, half-transparent, and you could see the brightness of the sun filtering through. When there was a little room to turn round in, Brinetta looked at me and grinned. 'Well, this is the market,' she said. (pp. 24–25)

Although the boy's initial confusion steadily gives way to an increasing confidence and pride in his marketing skills, and to his becoming in a sense a member of the market community, these developments are coloured for the reader by another complication. The boy's visits to the market echo his need to belong somewhere, against a background feeling (not so much recognized by as felt through the boy) for mankind's vulnerability in the face of time. Francis had first visited the market with Brinetta, an elderly woman already passing out of the story and out of life. It is around the memory of Brinetta that the new feeling begins to form:

> The vendors knew me well by now, and they could almost tell what things I came for, and how much I wanted, and the things Mrs Chandles liked best. It astonished me and pleased me very much that they should know this . . . They laughed all the time and they talked in Hindi to one another and they looked very nice in their saris and muslin veils. And mostly there would be gold-plated teeth in their mouths and heavy gold bracelets on their wrists and ankles. They were very pleasant to buy from.

Whenever they spoke in English it would be to ask me about Brinetta and I would say I did not know where Brinetta was. 'Where she garn,' they would press, 'you don't know where she garn?' And when I said no, they would shake their heads and look at each other as if to say it was very strange I did not know. They had never forgotten Brinetta. (p. 103)

And at the end of the novel when the characters are moving apart, with Mrs Chandles dying ('she travelling home') and Francis about to get his bus back to the village, Brinetta and the market become the means by which the boy knows, hardly knowing that he knows, that death is part of the streaming life he has entered:

Thinking of the market I remembered Brinetta and I was glad for remembering her now. For she slipped entirely from my mind. I thought, Look how Brinetta has gone away forever, and how I was leaving for good now and she wouldn't know, and she might never know Mrs Chandles died this year. (p. 135)

As the novel draws to an end, Francis has come to understand a certain section of San Fernando, an area of experience has been sounded. To the responsive reader, the end means more than this, but there is no attempt on the novelist's part to suggest that the boy himself has now 'reached maturity' or lost his innocence. Francis, indeed, is unable to pass judgemen' on the events and people that impinged upon his consciousness during the year in San Fernando:

The bus roared on and my mind went on Mrs Chandles, who was dying, and Mr Chandles – so strange of late, and now home-less; and I thought also of Mrs Princet, and I thought of Edwin and that dollar. I thought of all the mixed-up things, of all the funny things, in fact, which made the year at Romaine Street. (p. 137)

But it may seem at this point that we have been suggesting the superiority of the reader's vision to that of Francis, and if so, we should want to modify such an impression radically. We have already suggested that in this novel the author involves us in the feel of a peculiarly 'open' consciousness. It is 'open' in several senses. Because the novel is a work of memory, dealing with a single year in terms of a small cluster of places and repeated activities, it presents the boy's consciousness as a fluid condition in which different times, events and places co-exist. This is expressed over and over again in the boy's capacity for simultaneous recall and experience, and it is the source of the novel's seemingly accidental metaphors and natural symbolism.

The boy's consciousness is also open in the sense that it leads away from the stock response by seldom allowing conventional associations between the attributes of a person or thing and the interpretation of them. In the following paragraph, the boy's response to the 'ghoulish' Mrs Chandles is not the response to something ghoulish:

> ... Mrs Chandles thought I was smiling with her. She looked strangely pleased. Her smile had big pleats on the cheeks and under the chin and the flabby skin round her eyes were now a thousand tiny folds. Her gums showed pink and I could see the sockets and her eyes shone out like two jumbie-beads. It was strange, because she looked spooky somehow, and yet she looked so sincere, I believed in her. We smiled broadly. (p. 68)

The open consciousness responds to each experience in an immediate, excitable way. This extreme susceptibility leads the boy away from passing judgement, into making sometimes conflicting responses to the same thing or person from situation to situation.

The most prominent mark of this open consciousness in the novel is in the number of occasions when Francis experiences shock. The structure of the novel lends itself to this recurrent aspect of the boy's behaviour. What goes on away from the house is outside the boy's consciousness, but those who are involved in these actions (notably Mr Chandles) are in periodic contact with Francis. For this reason, Mr Chandles' return from Mayaro at midday on Saturday is a source of dread to the boy; his departure, listened for, brings great release: 'From where I was I could hear him brushing his teeth very forcibly, and I could hear the tap water running and being sucked down the drain. Then the water stopped running and I did not hear him for a little while. Then came his footsteps, and when the front door opened and shut again, my heart was pounding. The next moment the gate slammed. I was wildly glad.' (p 38) On one occasion Anthony uses Francis' unusually long absence from the house to great effect. The boy returns from his stolen visit to the sea to a terrific row between

Mrs Chandles and her son about Marva, the woman in Mayaro. Francis disturbs his routine, and keeps busy unnecessarily watering the plants on the veranda until the smell of the flowers makes him think about Mr Chandles' other girl, Julia, for whom Francis has felt the first stirrings of love and jealousy:

> I stopped a little and laughed at my silly thinking, and then I jumped because the front door was pushed open. Then I heard Mr Chandles in the veranda. His footsteps were sounding double, and when he came to the steps I straightened up and stood on the side, allowing him to pass. And then, turning round with the can, my heart gave a violent thump. Mr Chandles and Marva were going out through the gate. (pp. 98–99)

In so far as Anthony is able to involve us in the feel of an open consciousness, we are made to live in a world emptied of complacent existence so that we grope with Francis towards a 'meaning' for his experiences. As we have said, it is also part of the novel's technique that the reader should be able to 'recognize' some of these experiences over Francis' head. But Anthony is not interested in an ironic contrast between the boy's innocent vision and the reader's experienced interpretation. The story itself is a sordid one – a protracted squabble for the house between Mrs Chandles and Mr Chandles who wishes to take it away from his brother Edwin; a double love affair being conducted by Mr Chandles with Marva the girl in the Mayaro and Julia the girl in San Fernando; and the callous treatment of the young boy in the Chandles' household. How little Anthony is concerned with a moral judgement or indignant protest or other forms of opposition may be illustrated by the boy's changing perspectives on Mrs Chandles.

He first hears of her as 'old and lonely' and wanting someone to stay with her (p. 4); his first experience of her is as a remote voice (p. 12) and when he first sees her she is aloof and somewhat frightening: 'Mrs Chandles had stood up for a moment as if inspecting me. She was very old and wrinkled and small. The next moment she hobbled away through the door through which Mr Chandles had gone.' (p. 13) As the novel progresses Mrs Chandles emerges as demanding, cunning and nasty. After a row with Mr Chandles she locks herself in for the day and leaves Francis stranded ('. . . I wondered to myself what sort of human being this old lady could be. She hadn't cooked. She couldn't expect that I had eaten. She had left me to starve and like Mr Chandles she did not care a damn.' (p. 63) Yet Francis tries to please her and when Mrs Princet arrives to visit her girlhood friend, Francis enjoys Mrs Chandles' good humour as if her previous manner did not matter, 'My heart was light and as open as the skies in a way I had hardly known it before. This was an Easter Day beautiful in itself and beautiful because of Mrs Princet, and because of the strange kindness of Mrs Chandles. I thought I should never forget it.' (p. 53) Later, when the rains come Francis feels himself bound with an extraordinarily winning Mrs Chandles (pp. 78–91) who is now like a relative. When Mrs Chandles becomes ill and is dying the boy neither sentimentalizes her nor is vindictively joyful at her imminent death but becomes the agent of the novel's compassion.

By mid-December, with school having closed for Christmas, I spent the holidays being busy in the house. Mrs Chandles was – as the elderly lady said – just awaiting sentence, though I couldn't think what greater sentence could come to her now. But she was waiting all right. It was a strange how hard and untiring the elderly lady worked. For, as she said herself, all she was doing was in vain. I watched her rush in and out of the room, always with hot water on the fire, always with foul-smelling bed clothes to wash. And yet she did everything with zest. It was as if she was just getting the feel of the wrestle with death and was enjoying it. I thought maybe she had always been at the side of the dying. I thought maybe it made no difference to her if death won all the time. Mostly, I wondered how was she really feeling inside, and sometimes I thought to myself how much money could Mr Chandles be paying her. (p. 121)

The realism is not callous. Death is seen through the unblinking eye of the young boy as a messy and degrading business; not a remote and separate state but something all are involved in, and requiring neighbourly care which is far from including as it does the payment of wages to the elderly nurse, the washing of dirty linen, bad smells, skin and bones and a terror in the face of death:

Sometimes she called me to help her with Mrs Chandles and there was never anything like dismay in her voice. Whenever we were too slow and Mrs Chandles soiled the sheets, all she would say was, 'Look out!' after it had already happened. This amused me. Immediately she would clean the helpless sick, and getting me to help, she would hold Mrs Chandles to one side of the bed, then to the other, and like that she would put new, clean sheets on the bed. Holding Mrs Chandles was no strain for my arms and she felt just skin and bones. Anyway after putting on the clean sheets the dirty linen would be bundled into a cardboard box to be taken downstairs to wash. But before this was done, Mrs Chandles would be put to lie nice and comfortable on the bed.

At such times I had always tried to do what I had to do without thinking of the sick before me. For her eyes would be like death itself and her body would be as stiff as a board though it did not seem this was on her account. Usually she never seemed to know what was going on. And sometimes while I held her there amidst all the mess I felt as though the stench of the bedclothes was going to suffocate me.

And so looking on at these things I knew the end could not be far off now. I had seen only one dead person before, and thinking of that face now, and of this, it was striking how alike were the faces of death. I had gone to the house and had watched that dead man's face and was terrified. (p. 122)

Sentences like 'I thought she had always been at the side of the dying', and 'it was striking how alike were the faces of death' reverberate beyond their literal significance for the boy and take on an oracular meaning. The quality of human endurance illuminates the whole passage, though not in any romantic way through formal heroic or sentimental poses. The woman helper 'did everything with zest' yet the boy wonders 'how was she really feeling inside', and we are given an insight into this possible ambivalence through the boy's own responses – 'I had always tried to do what I had to do without thinking of the sick before me ...' but 'sometimes while I held her there amidst all the mess I felt as though the stench of the bedclothes was going to suffocate me'. The boy is learning about his own strengths and frailties within the processes of growth and decay to which he is discovering himself to be bound. In an adult observer, the tone of what Francis says might have appeared insensitive. But as the boy speaks, the reader knows what Francis is learning, and what lies ahead. Characteristically of the novel, the reader lives imaginatively the experiences of the boy, but is compelled to measure these experiences against his own maturity, the reverberations of the boy's words and the stark perceptions of the innocent eye.

To end, then, with a statement about character in the novel, we might say that *The Year in San Fernando* leads away from the notion of fixed personality or conventional ideas of character formation; and points towards a more liberal view of latent and sporadically realized possibilities. It is in this that we think the remarkable originality of the novel lies. The image of Francis, deprived and tethered to the Chandles' home (even to having a lair beneath the house) in a circumscribed world of which he is trying to make sense, in an image of the condition of the modern West Indian. But out of this distress Anthony has created an archetypal situation. On the one hand there is the pattern, of growth and natural progression, reinforced by the metaphorical activity of the novel's language; on the other, there is the narrator's extreme openness to the possibilities of experience, marked particularly by Francis' capacity for shock. Through the boy's consciousness Anthony leads the reader to acknowledge his own helplessness and perplexity, and to go beyond this to the continual transformation and re-creation of the unstable world:

I remembered walking through the short-cut in the heat of the dry season when the tall trees among the houses had been stricken and barren-looking, and had not caught my eye at all. I remembered seeing the mango – so sensitive to heat – and their leaves had been shrivelled up and their barks peeled, as if they had surrendered and could take no more. I remembered the cedar, too, one of the giant cedars, and I had even looked at it and thought how much firewood there was here. But all those trees had sprung to life again, with the rains, and were so rich in leaf now, it was unbelievable. But I had seen this myself. And now I watched the great cedars sending even more branches into the sky of the town. (p. 105)

ONE

We had heard only very little about Mr Chandles. The little we had heard were whispers and we didn't gather much, but we saw him sometimes leaning over the banister of the Forestry Office, and indeed he was as aristocratic as they said he was. He looked tidy and elegant and he always wore jacket and tie, unusual under the blazing sun. These things confirmed that he was well off, and his manner and bearing, and the condescending look he gave everything about him, made us feel that he had gained high honours in life.

Mrs Samuels of the Forestry Office must have been sure of this. She seemed to consider his week-ends under her roof very flattering to her. She seemed to have had no hesitation in approving the friendship between Mr Chandles and her precious Marva.

It was the whispers about Mr Chandles and Marva that we heard so often in our house. Ma worked for Mrs Samuels so it was expected she would know a great deal. She was cook, maid, butler, and even washerwoman, and therefore had opportunities to see and hear almost everything. Besides, she was Marva's close friend. It was surprising to know that Marva could have a close friend at all, or could confide in anyone, for she was vain beyond the telling. But she had fine looks – people said that about her. And now that a gentleman was visiting the Forestry Office, they said a lot more about her.

But Ma, who was without malice, thought the friendship a very nice thing indeed. Ma thought at last some person worthy of Marva had come along. Someone of Marva's high culture and education. Ma talked in that fashion all the time.

We often listened to this, and detesting Marva as we did, we often accused Ma of being more interested in the affairs of these two than they themselves were. Whenever anyone came home for a gossip the talk inevitably went on to Marva, and Ma always boasted about being Marva's close friend, and about what a fine girl she was, and about the costly things she had, and she talked about Mr Chandles' position at the Great Asphalt Company in La Brea, and about the loads of money he was making every month. This always made a great impression on the person she was talking to.

Sometimes it impressed us also. Indeed, this status of Mr Chandles must have been what was causing Mrs Samuels such elation. She had always, when she went walking, stepped out of the Forestry Office with decorum, but now this decorum was grossly overdone, and the way she swung her umbrella and held her head to one side offended the people a great deal.

So now there was no enjoyment in watching her pass. She had had the reputation of being the most elegant lady in the village – after Marva – and people had always made mention of her among themselves, and we had been proud that Ma was working for her and that we could go over to the Forestry Office whenever we wanted; not only to the office itself, where people went for passes to fell timber or cut thatcher leaves or on other forestry business, but to the house proper, and to the kitchen, where Ma always was. Mrs Samuels had always been glad of us. That is, until Mr Chandles came along.

And so Mr Chandles seemed to have suddenly changed all her grace and her simplicity and now we felt she was really complicated. Life, on the whole, became a little more complicated. The Forestry Office grounds had been fenced off with tiger-wire, and we often watched Mr Chandles leaning against the veranda rails, looking over the tiger-wire fence into our yard. Our yard was always untidy and the lime trees were untrimmed, and since Pa had died the grass in the yard was uncut, and around the mango tree it had grown rather tall without our bothering about it. We could see the look on Mr Chandles' face as he gazed over into our yard and somehow we felt rather small. He was so different by comparison. He was so tidy-looking and neat. It was impossible not to admire him. Really, it seemed wrong that people should speak so ill of him. As Mrs Samuels had said, they didn't know anything about him and they were nothing but a pack of gossip-mongers. She had said they were simply jealous of Marva. She told Ma several times that they were *jealous, jealous* of Marva, because Marva was not of their class and did not associate with them. Marva had nothing in common with them, she said. That was why they hated her.

To my own mind this seemed true enough. Of all the people in the village only Ma really cared for Marva. And of course, Mrs Samuels. And certainly, Mr Chandles. Mostly, people said they couldn't stomach her. She dressed, not extravagantly, but a little too well, and she spoke an English far beyond the range of us all. Indeed, she had nothing in common with the villagers and it was not only Mrs Samuels who knew it. Maybe it was true they were all jealous of her in some way. Now mischief flourished. Everybody knew what time of night Mr Chandles arrived in the village and how Marva went down to the bus-stop to meet him and how they walked up the road hugging up in the dark. Ma said as far as she knew Mr Chandles had never arrived in the night. Anyway that did not stop the gossips, and whenever the women went to the Forestry Office they looked at Marva in a very knowing way.

Mr Chandles was seeming to come more frequently as the days wore by and at home now there was much talk from Ma about the wedding to come.

Christmas just past and Mr Chandles had stayed a little while over the holidays. Looking towards the veranda of the Forestry Office we had seen quite a lot of him. Sometimes on going over to the Office on errands for the neighbours, we would see him behind the counter helping to sort out applications or talking to Marva. Those were the few times when we saw him near up.

But Ma saw him near up all the time. It even appeared that he was getting sociable with Ma. And it was just about now that the first big thing happened.

Ma rushed home from work one evening, very excited. Usually she'd walk out into the main road at the front and then come home, but this evening she just held the tiger-wire apart and slipped through.

'You know what happen?' she said, almost out of breath. 'You know what happen?'

We waited in suspense to hear, and my brother Felix said, 'What happen, Ma?'

'Hush up,' she said, 'I talking. Listen to me!' She did not say this unkindly but it was very irritating.

'You all know what happen?' she said.

We said nothing.

'Francis going to live in San Fernando.'

There was shock all round and all eyes turned on me. I was flabbergasted. I did not know what it was all about. And then Ma

3

began to explain. She started by saying that Mr Chandles had plenty of money and a big house in San Fernando. She said that some time towards the end of the year – the new year had just come in – he was going to marry Marva. But they were not going to live in San Fernando, she said. For the reason that Mr Chandles had a big job at the Great Asphalt Company in La Brea. they would live at La Brea, and only his mother would be in the big house in San Fernando. The mother was old and lonely and wanted someone to stay with her. She was a kind dear soul and just wanted someone to go to the shops and do little errands and everything else would be very nice. Ma said I was the lucky one because Mr Chandles could have got hundreds of little boys to go but he had asked for me, specially. She thanked God that I had come into such good fortune.

We, the children, were much too surprised to speak. Ma asked me wasn't I glad to go. I did not know what to say. Leaving home had never entered my mind. I had thought of almost everything, but not this. I had heard of San Fernando, the great town on the other side. I had never had to think of it very much. I had thought of it as I thought of many other things. I had never imagined living in it.

I was surprised to hear that Mr Chandles had asked for me, specially. I would never have believed it hadn't Ma said so. He had often caught me stoning the guava tree, and the way his eyes had fallen upon me I would never have thought he'd ask for me to live in his big house.

Anyway, when Ma had spoken, she stood there waiting for me to answer. She looked impatient and surprised that I did not jump at the great news. 'You want to go or not?' she said, 'Mr Chandles want to know.'

I looked at Sil then. You could never tell what Sil was thinking. He was my small brother but he was mostly sensible but now I could not read anything on his face.

Felix and Anna were all for my going. I could see that. They looked at me as if to say I was stupid and that Mr Chandles should change his mind, and that if I didn't want to go *they* knew of others who would.

While I sat there, my thoughts confused, Ma began praising Mr Chandles again. No one would have believed there was so much good in one man, but Ma went on talking. Then she changed to the subject of our own father, and how he died out and left her with

4

four starving children and how God alone knew how hard she was fighting to raise us. That was true. I knew that, for one thing. When Ma talked like that I knew how hard she was fighting. Mrs Samuels was very kind but nobody would believe it if you said how much she was paying Ma to do almost everything in that big house – to wash, starch, iron, cook, sweep-up, and to run errands – people would not believe it if you told them. But her money was keeping us from starvation. No one knew about the pay but people could not help seeing how Ma slaved. They said she would run her blood to water. Hearing this so often I seriously feared it would happen. I always thought, if it *could* happen, would it happen on of these days? I looked at Ma now and she gazed back anxiously, hungry for the word. I said, yes. She was almost beside herself with joy. She hurried down the steps and made for the Forestry Office.

Again, she did not go out into the road and enter the building from the front, but instead she ran towards the tiger-wire fence and held the spiky wires apart and eased through, then disappeared towards the back of the building. Her sprightliness amazed us.

I felt strange for most of that night and when I awoke the next morning I still felt strange. It seemed as though I was suddenly changed without and within. I could not be the same because I was going to San Fernando. I kept thinking about this and mostly I wanted to be myself. Every morning now, during the holidays, Sil, Felix and I played cricket in the road, but this morning I did not feel like playing any cricket, and I went to the back of the house looking down at the bushes. Somehow, the knowledge that I was going away made Mayaro look very strange. The lime trees looked greener, for one thing, and the sudden down-sweep of the land towards the ravine, rising again at the far, grassy hills, seemed to make the place look unusual this morning, and rare.

I did not know why this was so. I was sure it was I who was unusual for I was feeling that way inside me. Nearby, close to our pea trees, stood the giant guava tree, just on the other side of the tiger-wire. A great many of its branches hung over to our side, and they were laden with ripe fruit, and it was these that I often stoned, standing almost concealed between the pea trees.

I just didn't feel like stoning the guavas, this morning. I saw them and they meant little to me, and this was very unusual. Standing there I could hear the voices of Sil and Felix in the road, arguing as to who should bat first. Sil was always arguing about that. I was not even stirred to go and play cricket. I suddenly remembered school and how I would not be going back and I became alarmed. What would Mr Guilden say? Perhaps he would come home to see Ma about it. I wondered what the class would say. Then I remembered the term test. At the Christmas break-up we had not got any results. I wondered if Mr Guilden would send the results home to Ma, and I wondered what place I had made in the test.

And now, slowly, my thoughts shifted to the big house in San Fernando. I wished I had some idea of what it looked like. I wondered if it was as fine a building as this Forestry Office here. This was really a huge, great building. Terrific. As I turned my head to take in again the vastness of the Forestry Office, my heart almost leaped to my mouth. Just on the other side of the tiger-wire was Mr Chandles. He smiled with me.

TWO

I remember the journey to San Fernando mainly through Balgobin, who was conductor on the first stage – to Rio Claro. Balgobin was an old friend, and he spoke to me quite freely, and Mr Chandles kept looking at him in a certain way, and I could not answer Balgobin properly and I wished he would hush up. Balgobin was excited about my going to San Fernando and he asked me all sorts of questions although he saw Mr Chandles was with me. He asked me where was I going to stay and I tried to make him an eye to show I was going to stay with the person beside me, but he did not understand, and he said loudly, 'What happen, boy? You 'fraid to talk?'

This made all those at the front look round, and some laughed, and I was so embarrassed I could not look to see how Mr Chandles' face was. It was a very coarse crowd – as usual – and Balgobin spoke very coarsely, and I could guess what Mr Chandles was feeling to be sitting here. For he was refined, and from his very dress you could tell he was of a class apart. He said not a word and when Balgobin came to collect the fares he just dropped the money into his hand. Balgobin gave him his change, looking at me most of the time, and before he moved away, he said, 'Well, Franco boy, I may see you down San Fan one of these days. I know San Fan you know!'

I merely said, 'Yes.'

He looked shocked. 'You shame to talk to me?' he said, 'Well I never!' And he gave out a long, big cackle of a laugh, which made most of the people on the bus laugh too.

I felt so foolish I didn't know where to turn my head. I knew I was acting silly with Balgobin but I could not help it. I felt very odd because of Mr Chandles. I wanted him to feel I was of some refinement. And yet I wished I could be free with Balgobin. I felt so dejected, I was relieved when Rio Claro came into view.

When we left Balgobin and the Rio Claro bus depot behind, a storm of home-sickness swept down upon me. I felt finally cut off from Mayaro. I looked out at the town which was beginning to rush back outside. I didn't want to think of home itself just yet because it made me feel so odd to think of all of them fussing to see me go. I could hardly think about it without it making my eyes fill up. I looked out of the window and watched how the bus was going. This was a much more comfortable bus than Balgobin's. I had never been out of Mayaro before and so had never seen these yellow buses. The next stage would be Princes Town and we would get out there and change again. The sun was still hotly bright, and the trees and houses cast long shadows across the road, and I wondered what time would we get into Princes Town. And then Balgobin came to mind. We were often with him at the river. Sometimes he would chase us round to throw us into the deep part, but if he slipped and fell we would all get hold of him and throw *him* in. He was an amazing diver. He stayed so long underneath sometimes you'd thought he'd drowned, and . . .

The conductor's voice brought me back to the moment. He had only just come to Mr Chandles to collect the fares. He was a very placid conductor, much unlike Balgobin. He didn't joke with anybody. I looked outside again.

Rio Claro was still rushing back. Rio Claro was many houses edging on the sidewalk and some in the background wherever I could see, and also there were a few big roads leaving the main Princes Town road. We were speeding downhill now and on the right I could see the railway station lying back. No one had to point out to me that it was a railway station, although I had never seen one before. There was a long row of carriages, and the engine was smoking and the wind was twirling up the black smoke and blowing it over the houses. I saw this all in a moment and presently we were climbing a long hill, past a church, a Hindu temple, some ordinary houses, a school, other ordinary houses, and past another school with the sign saying: RIO-CLARO GOVERNMENT SCHOOL. The one before must have been the R.C. We sped on, with the traffic on the road being a steady two-way stream. This was a new strange world to me.

We passed cars and bicycles and big open-tray lorries and sometimes we went along with them. We went with some of them for miles and miles. We frequently crossed yellow buses, like ours, Rio Claro bound. They had PRINCES TOWN something or other written across their sides. We went quickly through this traffic and this road was not quite so bumpy although whenever we bumped we were thrown up from the seats. This was because this bus was very springy. Outside, houses had lined the road but now they were very few because we were drawing away from Rio Claro. We came upon water-taps along the roadsides and often there were girls filling their buckets and looking up to watch the bus pass. Sometimes they waved to the driver. Then presently we were out of Rio Claro and in open country. It was getting dusky outside now. There were not many big trees here and the land was rather open and in places where there were cane-fields I could see the reddish light among the leaves. And then I remembered something about cane-fires of which Balgobin had told me. But this could only be the evening light for it was not yet the cane season. This bus did not grate, like Balgobin's, but spluttered, and roared and sped on. And at times it went very quietly. Mr Chandles sat staring into space.

Night had already fallen when we arrived at Princes Town, and there we changed hurriedly for the San Fernando bus. This was to be the last stage of the journey. There were several buses lined up along the square and the one in front had people in it and its engine was running. We climbed quickly into the bus. I went into the seat first, so I had the window, and Mr Chandles sat beside me. My grip I had pushed under the seat and now had one foot touching it. I rested my arm on the little ledge beneath the window shutters and I felt really tired. I felt bewildered too.

8

For here was an even giddier world than Rio Claro. Outside, lights twinkled like candle-flies. Cars, bicycles, people, rushed about. The night was cool and it was pitch-black over the far houses. All around, cafés and rum-shops were open. The noises of people talking and the noises of cars and trucks and buses rose and fell but never died away. There was no silence here. At this hour, in Mayaro, most people would have already settled in for the night. Then, all that could be heard was the barking of dogs or the cry of a cigale or the winds in the trees. Here, life was not settling down for the night. Life was teeming. The night seemed to make no difference. Every moment I was blinded by the headlamp of some vehicle. The vehicles came roaring from the wide road ahead – the San Fernando road. The noises of the town rose and fell like waves running up and down a beach in the night. There were many people in our bus now. I was feeling tired. Just across the road there was a café full of people. Some were eating things and some had bottles of soft drinks held up to their heads. I was feeling thirsty for a drink. The noises rose and fell and the feeling was very similar to what it was when you were on Mayaro beach in the night. It was no use thinking about soft drinks. I wouldn't get one anyway. My throat felt dry. More people were coming into the bus. Outside it was like a carnival. Everything was so big here and so weird in the night. Some of the people from the crowded café were hurrying into the bus now. As soon as they got in they began grumbling that it was time to pull out. They were saying what time it was by the clock in the square. I couldn't imagine how anyone could see the clock in the square now. There was a little jerk. We were pulling out.

THREE

When we arrived in the great town, my head seemed to be spinning. The wide road from Princes Town had been filled with flashing head-lights and the roars of vehicles, and the roadsides had been strewn with villages – with sugar-cane fields between – and

9

finally there was the long bright village that lighted us into the town.

Now, tall, strange buildings towered high above the streets and under their overhanging verandas the pavements teemed with people. There were bright-coloured lights flashing on and off, and some flashed things about chewing-gum, and there was one that flashed 'ALWAYS OPEN', and there was the 'Drink Pepsi Cola', sign again. How many Pepsi Cola signs were there in the world? the thought came to my head. That sign was one of the first things I had noticed at Rio Claro. There was one even at Mayaro. In my jaded mind I thought of that girl drinking Pepsi Cola all over the world.

The streets were bright not only with the lights of vehicles, but with lamps hanging from streetside poles, and just next to one of these poles was a cinema displaying terrifyingly life-like pictures. I knew some of the names written on the pictures and I had recognized the face of one of the men who were fighting and covered with blood. Teelucksingh's travelling cinema used to come to Mayaro, and I had seen that blood-soaked man again and again. There was a little crowd of people in front of the cinema looking at the posters. Some were going inside. There seemed to be thousands of people about the streets. I walked close to Mr Chandles' side. A little way from the bus stop we turned off the main street, and then Mr Chandles spoke for perhaps the first time since we set out.

'Romaine Street,' he said.

It was strange to see the expression on his face now. He might have awakened from a long dream. Maybe it was the relief in being here that so brightened him. In the glow of the street-light I could see a certain warmth on his face. As he spoke, I could see, too, a look of surprise. Surprise, maybe, at my bewilderment – at my looking so lost in a place where it was natural to feel at home.

'You'll get to know San Fernando,' he said. 'Mother will send you round.' Then he looked back along the way we had come. 'Up there is the Coffee. The main street.'

'Yes,' I said.

'You'll have to open your eyes here,' he said, 'and watch the traffic. Here isn't like Mayaro, you know.'

'Yes,' I said.

I listened to him without strictly thinking of the traffic. It was strange to have him talking to me and with this town around me. I

10

had never thought there was such a place as this in Trinidad. Mr Guilden had never mentioned this in his talks on 'Our Island Home'. Mr Chandles had said one could get lost here so easily. Already I could see myself getting lost. I could see myself wandering hopelessly about this maze of streets. Listening to him, without considering the words themselves, I had the feeling things would be very mixed up when I went out.

We walked down Romaine Street and I watched the brightly lit houses on either side. There were coloured curtains hanging before the windows and the light that came from within took on the glow of the curtains. This made the street look very quaint. In some of the houses the jalousies were up and you could not see this, but where the jalousies were down or the windows open, you could see the coloured light filtering through, tinting the plants on the veranda rails, and on the concrete steps.

In the air was the faint sugary smell of the town.

We walked a little slowly because I could not carry the grip far without resting. I would have carried it on my head but Mr Chandles looked horrified when I attempted to do this. On either side of the street were pavements, and just where the street met the pavements, it sloped suddenly, and made drains.

I thought of Mr Chandles having talked to me. His voice had been friendly. This puzzled me a great deal. At Mayaro he had always been aloof and superior. Even on this long, strange journey he had hardly spoken at all. In his boredom he had slept a little part of the way. But he talked to me now. And his voice was friendly.

I walked near to him and I was glad. The grip was giving trouble and I changed it from one hand to the other, sometimes without stopping. I began to think of Mayaro a little and I began growing conscious of the loneliness closing in round me. I tried to keep out the lonely feeling because it was no good now and I walked close to Mr Chandles and I watched the brighter parts of the street where the street-lamps hung and I noticed how most of the houses were fenced round and some were open to the street without any hedge or fencing, and how the steps from some of them came almost right on to the pavement of the street. We walked down the left side of the street and then just before us was a big school.

The yard of the school was a little drop below the level of the street. The school stood a little way back and the yard was very

11

wide and seemed to sweep away in the half-light. The school itself covered a lot of the place and stood on tall pillars and I could see the side of the ground part was boarded round as if they kept classes underneath, too. We walked slowly and I was looking at the school and Mr Chandles said, 'Coffee R.C.'

I had already glimpsed that. The sign had stood out in the brightness of the street-lamp. I wondered what was Coffee Street R.C. doing on Romaine Street. And then I remembered that Coffee Street was that great road passing at the top. Many people were walking along Romaine Street. They talked and laughed and their voices came clear-cut sometimes, and sometimes muffled and clipped. We were still approaching the school and I was still looking at the weird empty yard when Mr Chandles spoke.

'You'll have to watch this school,' he said, 'This house here is yours.'

The house just before the school was journey's end.

FOUR

Mr Chandles stood up at the gate and rested down one of his cases and pushed the gate open. There were a lot of flower-plants along the veranda and along the sides of the steps. The plants along the veranda obscured much of the front of the house, but through the openings I could see there was light inside. We went up the front steps and into the veranda. Mr Chandles laid down his suit-case but the front door opened from within.

'Linden?'

'Mother.'

'Oh, it's you.'

'Who you thought it was!'

'Well I only said that. You bring the little boy?'

'I said I was going to.'

I was very puzzled. Mr Chandles seemed to be bristling. All this time he had stood up before the front door.

'All right, all right,' the old lady said.

Mr Chandles, still looking irritated, took up his things again. I was standing beside him, and with only one side of the front door open, I couldn't see clearly who he had been talking to. I was anxious for him to go in mainly so I could get a relief from the grip. I was a bit unsettled by the manner of the meeting between him and this person he called mother. It made me timid in a strange way. Also my mind was tired and giddy with the travelling. But I could not help thinking something was wrong between these two. I walked in behind Mr Chandles.

The light inside the room was dazzlingly bright. The first thing that caught my eye was the furniture – which seemed to take up most of the space – and the pictures hanging on the walls. Mr Chandles took my grip from me and went through the door straight ahead then closed the door behind him. Some of the chairs were like those newly brought to the Forestry Office – what they called 'easy-chairs'. These were cloth-covered and had cushions on them and looked very luxurious. I almost jumped at the old lady's voice.

'Sit down. Rest yourself.'

I was reluctant to sit on such fine-looking chairs but then I sat down. My eyes were burning a little from being suddenly in such bright light. Mrs Chandles had stood up for a moment as if inspecting me. She was very old and wrinkled and small. The next moment she hobbled away through the door through which Mr Chandles had gone.

I sat waiting. I could not remember sitting on any chair quite so soft as this one. I could not remember being in any place so grand and rich-looking. I had always looked upon the Forestry Office as a house of grandeur, but there was so much more grandeur here. For a moment I wished Ma was here to see, but then somehow I was not so sure. I did not know if things would go well.

I lifted my eyes to the pictures, which were very beautiful. Some seemed to be photographs, but most of them were oil paintings. In the far corner of the room there was a large box-like piece of furniture which I saw now to be a radio. I heard talking in the room ahead of me.

'Haven't fixed up anything yet,' Mrs Chandles was saying. 'Didn't know you'd get him. His things could stay here.'

Mr Chandles' voice made me wince. It was loud and sharp and angry. But Mrs Chandles seemed equal to it because her voice rose too. Perhaps she was used to it. She seemed hardened and used to many things. She had just given me one look-over and perhaps she was used to me now, too.

Mr Chandles came through this room again on his way to another room. He did not look in my direction. I sat there waiting for what I was to do next. Mr Chandles came out with a towel and soap-dish and other things and went through by the door ahead and after a while I heard a tap running. He called for something and the old lady went into the room he had come from. I sat there, feeling bewildered, trying to look at the pictures, trying not to feel so tired, and at the same time trying to follow what was going on. Mr Chandles went back into the room he had brought the towel and soap-dish from. His face looked smooth and fresh and superior. When he emerged from the room again he was wearing a different suit with one of those college things on the coat pocket. Once, when Balgobin wasn't in uniform I had seen him in a coat that had one of those things and he had said it was a monogram from the college. So far as I knew Balgobin had never been to any college. Anyway, Mr Chandles saw me sitting there, and he said, 'Mother'll fix you up.' Then he went out through the front door.

I did not see the old lady for a while. The door on the left of the drawing-room apparently led to the two other rooms. When Mr Chandles had opened that door I had glimpsed another door inside. It was his bedroom, then, on that side, and the room on the other side was the old lady's bedroom. The door ahead of me and opposite the front door led to the back part of the house. I knew the kitchen was that way, for I had heard the tap running. I was thinking of all this and trying to visualize the whole house from here, when Mrs Chandles came from the door ahead.

'You'll have to sleep here,' she said, beckoning to me. 'Mr Chandles ain't fixed up anywhere for you yet. You'll have to make it out here for the time being.'

'All right.'

I was looking on a much smaller room, which was neat and had nothing on its walls and had a big dining-table in the centre. My grip was leaning against one of the corners of the walls. There was a bundle of old clothing in Mrs Chandles' arms.

'You'll make up your bed with this,' she said.

'Yes.'

Her voice was a tremulous old lady's voice.

'What they call you?'

'Franco – I mean, Francis.'

'Francis?'

'Yes.'

She made a little scowl: 'Yes who?'

'Yes, Mrs Chandles.'

This unsettled me a little more. The old lady opened another door and this led into the kitchen. She opened several tins in the safe and in one of them there were some biscuits. She took out a few of the biscuits and put them on a plate on the tiny kitchen table.

'You from Mayaro?'

'Yes, Mrs Chandles.'

She pondered on it a little and somehow I felt Mayaro was a word that troubled her. She made some chocolate tea and poured some out and put it with the biscuits. 'Here,' she said, 'see what you could do with this for tonight. When you finish come in and shut the kitchen door.' She went back inside.

My head was too filled with the travel and the unusual sights and with the sense of being in such a strange house, to think much of the old lady. My heart, too, was very heavy. The biscuits were only a few but I could not eat them all. Outside I could hear the vehicles passing, and the voices of Romaine Street. I thought of the big school next door. I would see it better in the morning. Maybe I'd soon be going to that school.

Then my thoughts went to Mr Chandles. Just to see him about the house would have made me feel less desolate. He was my only link between Mayaro and this foreign world. He had been very civil to me walking from the bus stop, but on his arrival home he had become so different. He was his old self again. Also, at Mayaro he had spoken of his mother as 'dear', but now I saw there was open hostility between them. This shook me. Now he had gone out without even bothering to see me settled in for this first night. Heaven knew where he was, now, in this giddy town.

Feeling exhausted, I rested my head on the table and after thinking about Mr Chandles I thought of the place outside. Things were still passing in the road. Now and again I could hear the tooting of a bus and this probably came from the Coffee Street. My thoughts slipped into thinking of home. I wondered why really had Ma sent me here. They all said it would be very good for me. I wondered what they were doing over there now, if they were going to bed. It was about half-past nine now. They would be up for a long while yet. They would be talking of me, for sure. Maybe at this moment they were wondering if I was in San Fernando yet. I wished there was some way they could know.

All sorts of thoughts crowded into my head, but home stayed large in my mind. It stayed for a long time and I thought of Anna and Sil and Felix and of the neighbours and I thought of the Forestry Office and of the village itself, pitch-black in the night. And then the home-feelings eased away and thoughts of the big town came to me again. After a while this place might not be so strange to me. I might get to know it and maybe even to like it. But I did not know about that. It was hard to know about anything like that. But perhaps it would be good to get accustomed to the town and to get to know it so well that I could not get lost here. This house, too, was very fine. It had a rich appearance from outside and inside there were so many rooms and the walls were all painted and there was nice furniture, and pictures, and there was even a radio here. It was strange to be living in a house with all these things about. It didn't seem real to me and yet it was. Maybe after a while it would be as if I had lived here all the time. I might come to feel this my own home. I might even be able to play the radio whenever I wanted. Mr Chandles would seldom be at home. He would be mainly at the asphalt place. I couldn't be sure how long he would be staying here and how long he would be away. I was thinking about this when the door opened.

'Ready to come in?' the tremulous voice said.

'Yes, Mrs Chandles.' I got up from the chair quickly.

'Put the things in the sink. Don't worry to wash them up now.'

She was looking at me curiously. 'What you was doing so long? And you didn't even eat all the biscuits.'

'I was remembering home,' I said boldly.

She seemed to understand. 'Oh well,' she said, 'you have to try and forget home for now.'

We went in to the room where she had left my things. There was a pile of newspapers in one corner and the pieces of bedding beside it. 'See what you could do with these,' she said, 'for tonight.'

The old clothing had looked much more when I had first seen it. Some of it had even looked like good clothes. I wondered if she had suddenly remembered the newspapers and thought they would be just as good. I felt certain she had taken back some of that bedding.

16

I did not mind so much about sleeping on newspapers. Especially as it was for one night. I thought of using the little bedding there was as a pillow, and the rest would be the newspapers. That should be all right.

'And remember this is the dining-room,' Mrs Chandles said, 'I hear you does wet your bed.'

This made my heart jump. I did not say anything. She went out through the drawing-room and then I heard her inside a room which seemed to be just on the other side of the wall.

Most of the night I lay thinking. I could not go to sleep. This was not due to the newspapers, which were very strange to sleep on. They kept shifting whenever I turned and sometimes my feet were on the floor. But I was not greatly troubled by the newspapers. I could not sleep because the events of the day kept pressing upon me, and there was so much to think about. I lay wide awake, feeling so tired and yet not able to sleep and I stayed that way until finally the voices of the town went dead. Then it must have been the small hours of the morning.

Were it not for the newspapers under me, lying like this in the darkness and the silence was just like being in bed on any other night. Being in bed on any other night and just stretching my hand across I could touch Sil and Felix. Anna slept with Ma on the big bed. I would have been able to touch Felix and Sil now if this was any other night at home. Now I was alone. My heart pained me. I tried very hard to sleep but I kept turning on this side and that, and every time I turned, the newspapers moved away. It was uncomfortable in the extreme. The night was very still, now, and the air smelled of this house and of the town. I thought I would never drop asleep. My heart was very heavy. I lay with my eyes closed. I could hear a clock ticking somewhere. I thought I would never sleep.

FIVE

I was awakened by footsteps passing into and out of the dining-room. There were the noises of cup on saucer, of doors being opened and shut back hard, and of loud walking on the floor. The light had been switched on in the dining-room, too. When the footsteps came again I peeped from under my arm and saw Mr Chandles passing through. He went into the drawing-room and then I heard another door open. I heard him calling, 'Mother, Mother,' but not with any kindness of voice. She did not answer but I heard him asking for something. I did not hear what he asked for. Then the old lady's voice came sharply and angrily from her room: 'From the time you get up in this house of morningtime nobody can't sleep no more. The racket you causing! You ain't have no regards for nobody!'

His reply was even louder and angrier. He made it plain that he was his own boss and talking in his own house. Mrs Chandles flared up on this point and it seemed to reopen old wounds. There was mention of 'Edwin', and 'the old man', and the heated words went on for quite a while. Mr Chandles said she was stupid if she did not realize the house was his, and for years he had been paying all the rates, and neither she nor Edwin could shake him. Mrs Chandles said that with all the education she had given him he had turned out nothing more than an educated pig. He tried to shout her down, and in this early morning his voice seemed to make the house tremble. The quarrel went on in full cry and then it died down a little and Mr Chandles passed to and from the kitchen. He was without the little case he had been holding. He seemed busy and anxious to leave. Just as the quarrel seemed over, Mrs Chandles said, 'You think this is the Mayaro woman!' and the quarrel flared up again.

The old lady seemed to be getting the upper-hand now as Mr Chandles raced against time. I could see him through the narrow slit of my fingers which were over my eyes. He walked very

18

quickly in the house. Mrs Chandles went on with her tremulous screeching voice. It seemed once she had been stung into a quarrel she could not stop. She kept on about 'the Mayaro woman', and she said she didn't know why the hell he didn't stay there in the bush for good. And this other slut, she said, he could take her there, too, and let them both have it out down there.

I was astonished. I kept wondering who was the other one. I lay there with my eyes closed, listening.

Mr Chandles seemed harassed by this. He had just rushed out into the kitchen with papers in his hand and now he rushed back into his room again. You could see that he was in a hurry and that he was confused now. And yet again his voice came, ruthless and threatening. 'If it wasn't for one thing!' he said. 'God! If it wasn't—'

'Try it,' Mrs Chandles said, almost gently. 'Just try it.'

Mr Chandles' voice did not come again for a little while. His footsteps seemed to be all over the house. I heard him in the dining-room and it seemed he was walking slowly past my bed. I guessed it was to see if I was sleeping. I made my face as though I was in a deep fitful sleep. Afterwards, back in his own room, he said a few cutting words. I could hear how the voice was coming from the side of the drawing-room. He was saying, So help him, God, he would kick her out of this house. He said he was talking in cool blood but he meant it to the letter. Just wait and see.

He seemed to be looking all over the house for different things. He asked harshly where something was but the old lady made no answer. He went around pushing chairs out of his way. Every now and again there would be silence as if he stopped to think where the things might be. Then, from the sound of his walking, he went into his room. Presently he came out again and passed through the dining-room again, then I heard the tap running in the kitchen. When he came back I heard the old lady's voice in the drawing-room.

'You better tell the little boy all what he have to do.'

'He's staying with you, not me. You want this and you want that. You get a little boy now – *you* tell him what to do.'

'You responsible—'

'Responsible, my foot!'

There were crashing footsteps, then the front door burst open and slammed shut again, and Mr Chandles was gone.

SIX

That morning the odours of the town rose up strong and sweet. From the kitchen window I could see the fresh-looking red-topped houses trailing away towards the mist and the trees. As wide as the view would allow the town lay back, and I watched this, taking in the odours, and there was a smell of cane also. And I could see the cane-fields far away over the red roofs, half-green and half-white in the mist.

Up from the street that lay in the near distance and below, I could see vapours rising, and I could see that on the grass beside it, the dew had fallen heavily. There was no view of the Coffee Street from here, but the sounds of the heavy traffic, and the tooting of car-horns and bus-horns was very clear. And so were the many other noises of the town. For the whole place was coming to life now. First, on the street at the front – Romaine Street – there were the noises of car engines and bicycle bells and the talking of the early workmen. Then there was the bread-man. I ran out on the veranda when I heard him. I had just been taking up the news-papers I had slept on, ashamedly putting the wet ones between the dry, when I heard his singing. The bread-man had a huge donkey-basket on his head, and his voice was singing out, 'Bread basket, bread basket, a lovely morning basket!' I leaned over the veranda, my eyes straining to follow him. He soon passed from view.

I did not stay long in the veranda for I was already scared of Mrs Chandles. I went again to the back of the house, the bread-man's melody still in my head. Then I leaned over the kitchen window and looked around at the great strangeness about me.

Brinetta came in then. Brinetta was the old lady who called every morning to do Mrs Chandles' chores. She was, in a sort of way, an old friend. Usually she went to the market and helped to clean up the house and the yard. Mr Chandles gave her just a little pittance for this and she was going to stop. In fact, she had only been waiting until I arrived. She was wanting to go back to her village home.

So this week she was going to show me around. She was going to take me to the Corporation Market, and other important places, and give me useful hints. She was a small, crumpled-up, old lady, and though she looked very old she was much sprightlier than Mrs Chandles. When she smiled with me now her face seemed to make a million pleats.

'You is the little boy?' she said.

'Yes,' I said.

She looked me over, smiling all the time.

'Missing home?'

'Yes,' I said.

'Don't worry,' she said, 'you is a man. You'll be all right.'

Mrs Chandles must have known Brinetta was here for presently she came out with a list all ready for the market. Brinetta looked at the list, her head cocked to one side and she said what sort of cassava Mrs Chandles wanted? Mrs Chandles said, 'Well, after all, Brinetta, *you* know.' Brinetta pointed to me and said, 'Yes, but the boy don't know,' and she gave a little cackle of a laugh. Mrs Chandles lifted her eyes to heaven, and she said, 'All right, Brinetta, write in "butterstick".' Brinetta was still smiling. I thought Mrs Chandles had seen her point, somehow.

Brinetta made several alterations to the list and then she talked about things which were cheap just now. Mrs Chandles looked very interested. She said she was a woman who always bought quality and heaven knew she wasn't accustomed to counting pennies, and she mentioned something about the education she had given to Linden. At the mention of Linden, Brinetta's face changed. Mrs Chandles went to the cupboard for something and then she called Brinetta. I could hear them whispering from where I stood. I heard Mrs Chandles mention Mayaro more than once, and this did not surprise me for I knew who they were talking about. She went on talking in that tremulous voice and I could feel how bitter she was. But I could see Brinetta did not enjoy hearing these things. Her face looked even more crumpled now, and she kept turning her head from side to side, as if, from whatever way she viewed the matter, it disturbed her. Mrs Chandles did not take anything from the cupboard. She looked at me as though I had been standing much too close.

'You ready?' she said.

Before I could answer she said, 'Brinetta will do the market this morning. You going with her. You'll have to learn how to get so far by your own self. You could do shopping all right?'

I thought she said this last bit half kindly because she saw how confused I looked. 'Anyway put on your shoes,' she said, 'Brinetta will show you everything.'

I was glad and anxious to go out into the town. I put on my shoes. I saw myself in the big mirror through the open door of Mr Chandles' room. I felt I needed to comb my hair and change my clothes. I quickly went to my grip and searched right down at the bottom for my comb. Just when I thought it wasn't there I found it. I took out a shirt and a pair of trousers and immediately began to change. Mrs Chandles called impatiently from the kitchen as I hurriedly pushed down my shirt-tail into my trousers. Then I went to the kitchen. 'Changing clothes!' Mrs Chandles cried, shocked. 'Look here, boy!' she said.

'Come,' Brinetta beckoned to me, 'Let's run away quick and come back.' She went nimbly down the back step. I went out after her.

I felt she had called me on to rescue me from Mrs Chandles' harshness. But as she closed the front gate behind us, she said, 'When it's nice and early like this you don't have to worry about clothes. Nobody does notice you.'

She seemed clearly on Mrs Chandles' side. Yet she was so warm and friendly to me. I liked her in a sort of way.

I walked down-street beside her, looking at the big houses and breathing in the freshness of the town. It was very early, yet the sun was rising, and it seemed I could smell the flower-plants in front of the houses, and the streets were alive with many things. There was a man with a box-cart selling shaved-ice, and above his voice I heard the voices of small boys – young singing voices – crying, 'Guardian! Guardian Papers!' Now and again they came into view and they had large bundles of newspapers under their arms. They approached everyone in sight.

Brinetta pointed out several things to me. There were many cafés but they were not yet open. The whole place smelt of early morning and I felt bright and glad to be up. There were many street-sweepers at work and they exchanged greetings with Brinetta as we went along. From Romaine Street we turned into Cascade Street, and here the road was very wide, and the houses were big and strange and nice to look at. We turned up the street, and behind us and beyond, the road, declining, swept away to far houses, much like Romaine Street. Walking quickly beside Brinetta I looked around me a good deal. I noticed that it was the Coffee Street passing before us, right at the top, and I spotted many buses in the melée of traffic up there. Brinetta did not say anything for this little while. I watched the houses along where we walked and in some of them there were dogs sleeping in the verandas and there were little board-stands along the veranda rails, which, like ours, were packed with flower-plants. Fascinated, I looked at the Coffee Street again, at the stream of passing vehicles, and at the red roofs of the shops. And it was only after all this that I saw the hill.

'A mountain,' I gasped.

'It was there all the time,' Brinetta laughed.

I was taken aback at the Mount Naparaima of which we had all learnt at school. It stood towering like a great giant over the town, and I wondered how I did not look that way before. Now Brinetta touched me to show we were turning off the road.

We turned off into a little track which Brinetta called 'the shortcut'. I noticed she kept glancing back and there seemed to be something on her mind. Then she stood up and I stood up too. She said, 'You see that house over the road there?' She was pointing one way and looking another. I said, 'That house over there?' and she said, 'Yes.' She said that was the house that was helping to send Mrs Chandles to her grave. I did not understand and she did not explain, but I could see she was very upset about that house. She spat into the drain quite violently and we went along the track. She said I'd see and hear everything in good season. She didn't mind the one in Mayaro, she said, because that was the first one, and after all, a man must have a woman, but when it came to people cheapening themselves just for money, well! Then she turned round to me. 'You see Mr Chandles nice and decent, eh? Nice and decent! You don't know what a bugger he is!'

Somehow I wanted to laugh. Brinetta was so open with me that I was not embarrassed. I found myself wondering what was this other one like.

We hurried on. From the track we came into de Berrio Street, and from de Berrio Street we turned into a place which was the backyard of a number of ramshackle houses, with the ground stony and full of broken bottles and with the smell of soap-water and urine all round. Brinetta walked surefootedly on this difficult

23

ground and it was not easy to keep up with her. The ground sloped badly in places, and the splinters of bottle seemed to await the careless step. We passed a house where there were several old biscuit drums leaning up against a coconut tree. There were a few charred logs lying by on the ground, and there was a big rusty boom-kittle under the house. Before I asked Brinetta about this, she said, 'This is Steelband Yard.'

'O yes?' I said.

'All the big bands does come and practise here.'

I tried to think of all the big-band names I had heard about as we carried on among the rubble. There was 'Southern Symphony', 'Free French', 'Bataan'. I could hardly think of this and walk through this place. I hoped Brinetta would find no more short-cuts. Now there were little rubbish dumps and sardine cans all about one's feet and Brinetta was walking so fast I could hardly keep up with her.

We crossed Cipero Street and were back into similar surroundings and I was glad when at last we got out of that place. Standing on the pavement and waiting to cross the road I took in several deep breaths of the pure air. As soon as there was a break in the traffic we crossed and found ourselves in Keat's Street.

This was by far the busiest place I had seen. There were thousands of people about, and as most of them had baskets in their hands, I knew the market was nearby.

From the movement of the crowd I could tell the market was at the first road junction. Keat's Street carried on in grandeur and there were tall trees between the houses, and there was a hill with iron railings all the way along it. Within the railings I could make out things like crosses and there was a big statue of Christ looking towards us. I was not interested in burial-grounds.

At the corner, Brinetta took hold of my hand and steered me through the mass of people. We entered the great market building and walked full into the smell of chives and thyme and fruit and peppers and roucou and the freshness of fish and heaven knows what. As we joined the insurging crowd there was another tide pushing its way out. It seemed impossible we should ever get in but Brinetta seemed to be sliding through, and dragging me along. Soon we were well into the market.

The vastness of this interior bewildered me, and also I was amazed by the great mass of people and by the steady roar of human voices which startled you because you saw no one screaming. The roof was all slate, half-transparent, and you could see the brightness of the sun filtering through. When there was a little room to turn round in, Brinetta looked at me and grinned. 'Well, this is the market,' she said.

SEVEN

Before the end of that week I learned many new things about the town. I also learned my way about Romaine Street, and the surrounding area, and, now that Brinetta was gone, I went to the market all on my own. When I came back from the market I went upon the Coffee Street to fetch the special groceries Mrs Chandles wanted. Returning home from the shopping, there would be so much to do, that the day would pass quickly, and the time was very full.

Now, in this quiet moment of sweeping up underneath the house, Brinetta kept coming to mind. I liked her for many things, but specially for the way she spoke to me. No grown-up had ever spoken to me as if I could understand anything. But Brinetta did. Now she was in her village place. I felt sad.

That last evening when she had come to say good-bye I could hardly believe she was really going. The next morning she had not turned up and I felt there was a great emptiness in the house.

Now I got up and tried to finish the sweeping. Whenever I sat down here, in the morning, I felt so comfortable it was hard to get up again. This house was high enough for me to walk under it, upright, and its concrete pillars were as vast as those of the Mayaro Forestry Office. It was pleasant down here, and I was all to myself, and I felt reluctant to go up again and do the chores within.

This was so unlike going out into the streets. Going out into the streets was the greatest exhilaration for me. For me, there was still a quaintness about the town, and even along the market road, each day revealed new things. I got up early on mornings and changed and Mrs Chandles gave me the list and I went out into the sharp

25

keen air. The mist of morning would be so low you could hardly see the Naparaima Hill. I would walk very briskly, taking in the noises of the stirring town. On Cascade Street, the house that troubled Brinetta would always be closed and shuttered up – as if, indeed, its secrets, were many and evil and must be hid – but at that hour most of the other houses would be shuttered too, and I crossed into the little track without much suspicion.

Sometimes I walked in the centre of the track and sometimes on the grassy edge until I got into de Berrio Street. I always dithered along de Berrio Street. People seemed to get up earlier here, and even at that early hour there would be laughter ringing out from the houses. Sometimes I watched the men standing in front of these low houses, nailing up pieces of furniture, or doing things to the doors. At time their voices came loudly from the back-yards of the houses. Theirs were deep lusty voices, sharp and full of life.

The women here were mostly fat, and often they cooked meals on coal-pots in the open verandas. Their heads would be tied with red headcloths, or white, perhaps, and their faces would look round and happy and they would be chanting some strange tune in the drawling Baptist way. De Berrio Street seemed to be different from all the other places I had seen.

When I got to the market itself, the big lorries would be backing up to the gates, and market policemen would be directing them, and the vendors would still be unloading things from the lorries and vans and carting them to their stalls. The vendors came from the surrounding countryside, and among them were lots of Indian women with saris and Indian men with loin-cloths, and these, ac-cording to Brinetta, were mainly the melon growers from Penal. Their stalls were heaped high with water-melons and the young girls smiled at you so you'd come and buy.

I was beginning to learn the ways of the market and most times I bought things cheaply and had extra money left. With this I sampled the water-melons or pomerac or balata. Sometimes I bought barah and channa from the Indian women and they laughed to see how I enjoyed it. And sometimes they said, 'That bwoy, eh! I don't know! Every marning!' And I watched them smiling, their gold teeth glittering in the morning light.

Most of my little earnings came from the fish stalls. Mrs Chandles liked red-fish because it was a clean fish, she said. It lived at the bottom of the sea and it ate only moss, so it was very clean.

Never bring carite into the house, she always said, that was a carrion fish. But red-fish was very good.

But they seldom had red-fish at the market and indeed it must have lived at the bottom of the sea, so rare was it. When they brought in small quantities to the fish stalls the people who clustered around could not buy because it was too expensive. It was the only fish not on schedule so the price was 'wicked', as the housewives said. But Mrs Chandles must have it any cost. She boasted she was a clean woman and the red-fish was clean so she must have red-fish. I paid the price of the fish and when I got home I told her how much it cost, it being so rare, and the difference between the real price and the price I told her, gave me the pleasure of water-melons, and mangoes, and channa, or anything I liked.

Learning the ways of the market so well, and learning the ways of Mrs Chandles, I usually made a success of the shopping. Often Mrs Chandles was surprised at the things I brought back for the little money I spent. She became so pleased with my going to the market, that I suspected she was glad to be rid of Brinetta now. She didn't seem to miss her the slightest bit, now that she was gone.

The market crowd had been thick one Saturday morning, and it being so difficult, then, to get from one stall to another, I was late. I walked quickly back through the Steelband yard and along de Berrio Street, and as I crossed into Cascade Street I heard someone call my name.

'Francis!'

I stopped. It was a voice from that house which Brinetta had referred to. They knew my name. I was astonished. I walked a little way back and stood up on the side of the road, just outside the veranda of the house. The lady was leaning against the banister and smiling at me.

'You call me?' I said.

'Yes, I call you. How you like San Fernando?'

She was so slim and delicate that her dress seemed to drape round her, but she had a nice face, and her hair was combed up in the 'rose' style. It made her look – not glamorous – but extremely comely.

I did not know what to answer about how I liked San Fernando. I just said, 'It's nice.'

'Oh, it's nice?' she said. She stressed upon those two words as if those very words committed me. 'It's nice, is it? You like it?'

'Yes,' I said.

'And Mayaro – you don't miss Mayaro?'

'Yes,' I said.

She did not seem disappointed by this. She was smiling down at me as if it was a long time she had not seen me and was glad to see me again. Her eyebrows were thick and black and her eyes themselves were large and black, too, and she seemed all laughter and full of verve.

'San Fernando is a terrible place,' she said. 'Awful. But it's all right. Once you get to know it, it's all right.'

I wanted to say that I was getting to know it already and that it was all right. I wanted to say that I had just come from the market all on my own. Thinking of market, though, made me remember how late I already was, and how furious Mrs Chandles might be.

'Have to go,' I said. I wished I could say things nicely, as she did, but these were the words that came.

'All right then. You must come across sometimes. Mr Chandles coming today?'

It was then that it flashed to me that being Saturday, Mr Chandles would be coming today. Mrs Chandles had said they worked half-day on Saturdays at the Asphalt Lake and Mr Chandles was coming. Even before I had left for market she had been busy cleaning up and replacing things she had removed from their usual places. During the week I had missed the big clock from the drawing-room and I had seen her bringing this out of her room, dusting it, and murmuring things to herself. I could not understand how she could be so fussy about him, after all that had happened. That had riled me.

'Yes,' I said to the lady. She was not 'lady', really – she was little more than a girl. You could see she could not have left school a long time. 'Yes – I think so.'

'Well perhaps it may be nice for you, eh? You glad?'

'Yes,' I said. But I knew I did not look it. This girl seemed glad about everything. Perhaps it would be nice for *her*, I thought.

'Okay, then, Francis, if you have to go. You must come to see us, please.'

I felt very embarrassed about her saying 'please'.

'Okay,' I said.

'Okay?'

'Yes.'
'Cheerio, then.'
'Cheerio.'
'Cheerio, then.'

EIGHT

It was not easy to think whether I was glad to see Mr Chandles, or not. He was the only person in San Fernando I could say I knew. For I had been seeing his face for so many months, maybe a year. Sometimes when I had thought of Mr Chandles I had thought of him in that familiar setting. I had seen his face – not here amidst this maze – but leaning over the banister of the Mayaro Forestry Office. Mainly, when I had pictured him, I had pictured him looking over the tiger-wire fence into our yard. And at such times, in spite of all, I had a yearning to see him. But at other times, when his presence was more life-like in my thoughts, I was afraid, and shrank from him.

So when the car pulled up in front of the house, around midday, I stood in the backyard and watched. Mrs Chandles shouted to me to go out and help Mr Chandles with the things. She was supposed to hate him. I could not understand it. I walked out slowly to the front.

The car was just driving away when I arrived at the gate. Mr Chandles, tall in all his smoothness and tidiness, pushed the gate open.

'Afternoon, Mr Chandles.'

I was wearing the khaki pants of my brother which Ma had given me at the last moment. Felix had almost finished wearing them out and they were threadbare at the legs. I had been wearing them all the week and the dust from underneath the house had discoloured them. Mr Chandles looked at the pants, then at my shirt, then at my face. Then he snapped: 'Look at your condition. What you doing out here at the front?'

'Come to help with—'

I was going to say I had come to help with the things, but all he had in his hands was a little leather case. I was dismayed. I retreated to the back, passing underneath the house. I stood up for a while under the house and listened. My impulse was to be as scarce as possible. Then I thought I'd better go in and change these clothes. On second thoughts I decided I wouldn't change unless he told me to, because I wasn't anxious to annoy Mrs Chandles. She had threatened that if I kept on changing there'd be no laundry – I'd have to wash my clothes myself. She had said she did not like vanity.

I stood up among the tall pillars not sure of what move to make. Then I sat down on the old box and relaxed myself a little.

Presently there was talk going on upstairs. I heard Mr Chandles ask if the boy kept underneath the house clean. I did not know what the old lady's reply was, but after a while I heard him walking through the corridor beside the kitchen. I got up from the box I was not scared by his coming down to see how the place was swept. I knew if I had ever done anything well I had swept underneath the house well. The first time, Mrs Chandles wasn't too pleased and I had to do it again. Then I had taken my time. I had sprinkled the place with the watering-can to keep the dust down and had made the place all but shine. Then I had cleaned up the backyard and the space between the house and the fence. I had uprooted the stubborn sweetbroom, sending the snails crawling in all directions, and I had even curbed the cactus hedge that over-hung from the school side. To Mrs Chandles' horror, they had kept dances in the school occasionally, and the hedge had been stuffed with paper cups and paper plates and soiled handkerchiefs, which I had removed.

When Mr Chandles walked down the back steps now I slipped out to the front again, behind the flower-plants.

Presently he walked up the back steps again and apparently he had nothing to say and I heard him walking through the house. I passed back under the house and went indoors. Mrs Chandles hurried about the kitchen and I knew she was trying to get Mr Chandles' lunch quickly. Mr Chandles came into the kitchen and said something about shaving before lunch and the old lady began busying herself about his shave. I stood around trying to do something but there was nothing to do. I fidgeted about uneasily trying to appear busy, and Mr Chandles cast a few inquiring glances at me whenever he encountered me. I thought again of making myself scarce. I could not take my eyes off Mrs Chandles hobbling about. The truth was, she sickened me. It was hard to picture anyone more foot-kissing. Mr Chandles paid not the slightest attention to her.

Just to be out of the way I slipped out and went downstairs again. I thought of all sorts of things. I felt a quiet hate pouring into my head. I didn't know why this was so, because nothing special had happened today. I just felt I hated those two upstairs more than anything else in this world.

Then my mind went to the house on Cascade Street. I did not quickly get over the surprise of that girl knowing my name. Somehow I did not think it could be her whom Brinetta had spoken about. Still, she did not seem to dislike Mr Chandles. She had said, 'Mr Chandles coming today?' And her smile had been the smile of playfulness and expectation. I could not understand how anyone in the world could regard Mr Chandles with playfulness and expectation. I knew Marva did, but Marva was odd. It could not be this pleasant cheerful girl that Brinetta meant. I must have been mistaken.

I heard his voice upstairs and the thoughts stopped short. I began to ask myself why was I afraid of him. I felt glad to be here under the house. Now there were the heavy footsteps above. At times it felt as though the big feet would crash right through the floor-boards to the ground below. He did not wear iron boots but it was easy to imagine he did. This manner of walking angered Mrs Chandles too but she talked about it only when he was away at the Asphalt Lake. To be fair, she had talked about it when they had had that row that morning. Those two! I thought. At least Mr Chandles would be away again on Monday morning. That was something to look forward to.

I tried to ovecome my dejection. I tried to reason out why I was feeling so badly. I supposed I had expected some friendship from Mr Chandles. Perhaps one should not ever expect anything. Brinetta had said it was proper to stand on your own two feet and be good for yourself. Maybe one should be like that. The only thing was, I did not like the fear that was inside me.

At that moment, there was not much going on upstairs. The sun was very hot outside and the shadow of the house was very sharp and dark against it. From where I was sitting the profusion of flower-plants made a curtain between the house-front and Romaine street. On the other side the cactus hedge gave glimpses of the school.

The dejection was almost gone, though at intervals the realities of the house kept coming to my head. I had already found out a great deal. You find out too much! I told myself. And then I remembered Brinetta's favourite advice: *Take it easy.*

But the realities were in my mind. It could only be jealousy and selfishness that caused Mrs Chandles to hate Marva, for she knew hardly anything about her. She tried to get what she could from me. She didn't get much. I was self-satisfied about this. You're good for yourself already, I thought. I laughed quietly.

There was a little shuffling upstairs, and that was the old lady. Although I came to know a lot, I realized there was much I did not know. I thought, if it was her house, why didn't she throw him out, instead of fawning on him? The other brother would pay the rates and bills since he was so loving. He could have even moved over. Also, I thought, since Chandles had such a good job and so much money, why did he not clear out and leave her alone? There must be a lot I did not understand.

Sitting here on the box beside the pillar I did not try to understand. I just did not want things to worry me. I told myself that I was already twelve and I could do without letting these people worry me. Maybe if I worried them enough they would send me back to Mayaro. My longing for home was a great pain in my heart. I did not want to think of home now. I tried to drive away these seeping thoughts for they always made me feel in such a way I could do something desperate. I began thinking of the girl and at once I became cheered. She had big eyes and thick eyebrows and her hair was combed same as Anna liked it. But though Anna was my own sister and flesh and blood, and though she looked very nice with her hair combed that way, I would still put this girl miles in front. For her whole self, she was very pleasant to see. I wondered if she knew Mr Chandles well enough to think highly of him. She looked so simple and innocent I guessed she would think highly of anyone. I could see the girl-ness in her and somehow I could still see her in the way I could if I were grown. I could see her as being very pretty and if I were grown I would certainly ask her for us to get married. I felt strange thinking this way. She would probably laugh if any man asked her for them to get married. She might say she'd only just left school. I wished she did not want to get married to anybody. I liked her.

She and Brinetta were the only two friends of mine here. Of course Brinetta wasn't *here* anymore. She was gone and nearly forgotten. In spite of her helpfulness and her wisdom. Where did she go to again? I thought. I could not remember. Where was it she—

'Francis!'

I jumped up from the box, my heart giving a terrible shake and pounding against my chest. I did not hear when Mr Chandles had walked down the front steps. I turned round to him and I was speechless and afraid.

He approached me, the anger almost distorting his face. 'That is what you come to this house for!'

I did not say anything.

'Listen,' he wagged his finger close to me, 'Your mother said you wasn't lazy. If you think I brought you here to feed you and clothes you for you to idle under this house, I'll teach you! I'll pack you right back in the bush!'

'I does do work sometimes,' I said, tremblingly, 'I doesn't always come under here.'

'What sort of work you does do here,' he said acidly. 'From the time I come home today you under the house.' Then his voice rose sharply, 'You living under the house? Listen, if next week-end I come back and hear you still the same way – *out* you go!'

At the word 'out', I jumped, for he almost screamed it as he flung out his hand to show the severity of my being thrown out. He didn't say any more. He turned, and bending to avoid the rafters, he walked from under the house towards the front. Then he opened the gate and was out in Romaine Street.

NINE

I went towards the back of the house, then up the back steps. Mrs Chandles wasn't about. I went into the kitchen and drank some water, Mr Chandles was probably in her room. Outside it was hot and very bright and from the kitchen window I could see the sun glinting against the panes of the far-off houses. I did not remain at the kitchen window. I wanted something to do. I didn't want him to find me idling any more. I could not reason why because I knew I wanted more than ever to be sent back home. Yet I did not want Mr Chandles to come upon me idling. I was terrified of him.

I went and knocked on Mrs Chandles' door. 'Come in', she said. I went in and asked if there was anything around for me to do. She was half-sitting, half-lying in bed and now she shook quite distinctly. 'Listen boy!' she shouted. 'You is the devil or what. You better go and wash up the dishes or something!'

I hastened out of the room. One of the things I had noticed in the kitchen was that there were no dishes in the sink. Yet dinner was past. I knew Mr Chandles had eaten and she had eaten, and I knew where my food would be in the cupboard. Only that I wasn't hungry and would not eat now. Coming back into the kitchen I noticed all the dishes turned down on the place over the cupboard. Mrs Chandles had washed up the dishes herself, no doubt to show Mr Chandles that even this she had to do. So there were no dishes to wash up. I wondered if she had forgotten she had done them or was she just plain crazy. Then I heard her door creak open. She appeared.

'Scrub the passage,' she said, and hobbled back in.

I went outside for the pail and floorcloth. I was silly to think I would be idle. I would not be idle here. Not if Mrs Chandles could help it.

It was late evening when I finished all my work. Then I went and ate. The food was so delicious. I was very hungry, and very tired too.

There were a few things in the sink to wash up now and I did that and a few other things and I noticed night was coming on outside. Mrs Chandles was still asleep. I made sure I did everything I had to do, then I went to where my things were and took out an old reading book. I sat down at the dining-room table. If Mr Chandles came in and saw me reading let him see me reading. I sat there with my book but I was still uneasy and I kept myself alert for any footsteps coming up at the front.

After a time I heard Mrs Chandles stirring. She put on the light in the passage. The floor was still wet and I had scrubbed it very clean. Mrs Chandles went into her room again and she came out through the other door by the drawing-room. Then she closed the door that shut off the drawing-room from the dining-room. When she did this, it meant it was bedtime so far as she was concerned. I began feeling that way myself. I got up and started preparing for sleep.

Quickly I was finished and I took the light off. Lying down, fully stretched, I felt the house very quiet. Mrs Chandles seemed to have finally settled in. This was the peace on which my mind skated to places far and wide. Most times my thoughts went to Mayaro and stayed a long time there, and sometimes they went in search of Brinetta and found her wherever she was, usually in strange old places, her eyes peeping out from the wrinkles of her face. And sometimes my thoughts pondered here on this house and on Mr Chandles and this mother of his, and often I remembered what Brinetta had said, that the old lady really wasn't so bad, it was the old age.

I centred my mind on the place I was sleeping in. The things in this house were so many and of such richness. There were nice pictures and nice cabinets and there were new-looking chairs in the drawing-room. The way Mrs Chandles looked after them made me think they had cost a great deal of money and I knew they were very close to her heart. There was the radio, too, of dark-brown mahogany and so precious looking, and only this noon – since Mr Chandles had come – I had heard it play.

There were so many other nice things in the house, not to speak of electric lighting and water being actually indoors, that thinking of this now, I knew there was prosperity here. Of course, all over the town there seemed to be water and electricity in the houses, but in this house everything seemed to be of great value and well laid in. There was much more in any of these rooms than there was in all our house at Mayaro. In any case it was ridiculous to compare our house with this one. And yet in all this splendour I slept on the floor. This did not matter really, I thought. Then I began to think of how much money Mr Chandles must be getting per month.

Lying in the darkness with the air still and the thinking so pleasant, I felt quite excited to let my mind roam over the town. I thought now of the giant Mount Naparaima, and I was going to write a letter to tell them at home about it. If I did, I would put in about the mist at the top. I thought, too, of the maze of far-away houses bordering on the cane-lands and I tried to picture the winds of morning sweeping over the young cane, blowing the mists into the town. From the street outside, but mostly from the kitchen window, I had looked across the houses to where the town seemed to end and the fringes of green began. Mrs Chandles, in one of her few cheerful moments had told me that out there was Navet. She had pointed to where the houses began to dwindle, and there, you could see the town disappearing between the trees.

In my fancy I saw all these things now. Then I thought of the sea. I thought of the sea with some strange feelings because I could not imagine a sea that would not be crashing and tumbling like the one at Mayaro. The 'Little Folks' Geography has said the Gulf of Paria, being sheltered, was very quiet. In another part it had said the Gulf was *serene*. I could not picture this, but here the sea would be like a large pond, serene and dreamy, as when one was lying down on a bed at night. Also, there was a wharf at the waterfront. Brinetta had spoken of it and she had spoken of the jetty beside the Harbour Master's place. I lay now seeing it all in my mind. My thoughts floated far. I must have dropped asleep soon afterwards.

TEN

A few Sundays afterwards, I was awakened early for market. The market opened at five on Sundays and there were always big crowds. When I left the house it was still chilly from the morning wind. I shivered and walked very fast.

I remembered that Mr Chandles was in the house when I left. He was in the kitchen when I had to go there for the basket and I was afraid to attract his attention and at the same time I was afraid not to say good morning to him. So I had gone timidly and unhung the basket and had said, 'Morning.' I did not know whether he heard or not. I had moved off quickly after that.

In the market itself I lost no time. There were huge crowds. I eased my way from stall to stall and I thought I did good business. There was good veal at the beef-stalls and I bought from the vendor I liked, though I did not know why I liked him. He looked at me now as though he recognized me.

I took no notice of the fruit and melons today. I could not risk any extra pennies. I hurried to get the things I had on the list, at the same time being careful of what I bought. When I arrived home again Mrs Chandles could not hold back her surprise at my being so quick, and at the fine shopping I did. I watched her face as she put the things on the table and she looked very pleased.

The rest of the day seemed without end. I spent my time trying to avoid Mr Chandles and yet I was afraid to be caught under the house again. So I stayed indoors, feeling confused and wanting something to do.

I had hardly seen Mr Chandles' face all day. We met in different parts of the house but I got out of his sight as quickly as possible. When he came into the kitchen and I was doing chores there my heart beat very fast and I tried not to let my eyes meet his and all through this I felt terrified inside. And to my surprise, towards evening he spoke to me. He called me into the drawing-room and said: 'Well, you'll have to start school soon.'

I didn't know what to say.

'Not this school here,' he said. 'You'll go to the Government school. You'll have to do some work at Government School – not play, play, play, like over there.'

As he talked he looked rather cheerful. 'All right?' he said.

'Yes,' I said.

'Okay, then, well that's that.'

I had known I'd have to be going to school some time, because in San Fernando it was the law, but I did not guess I'd be going very soon. I at once started day-dreaming about school. I did not know how it was to go to a new school in a new town. But I knew how it was to go in a new class on the first day after the holidays. I liked that and it was very strange. Everybody had new reading books and I liked the smell of new reading books when you opened them. The girls always looked cheeky in their ribbons and bright dresses, and they looked strange and grown for being away so long, but the boys looked as though you had been seeing them all the time.

I was excited. I did my work with vigour that evening. And towards evening I had a glimpse of Mr Chandles all dressed up, and my heart lifted. He was going out. I was glad he was going to send me to school, but I could not help feeling the great relief to know he was leaving the house. I was always tense when he was by. When he left the front door I would feel as if the world had suddenly broken loose about me. I was over-anxious for him to go out now because I wanted to feel this way and to think about going to the Government School. From where I was I could hear him brushing his teeth very forcibly, and I could hear the tap water running and being sucked down the drain. Then the water stopped running and I didn't hear him for a little while. Then came his footsteps, and when the front door opened and shut again, my heart was pounding. The next moment the gate slammed. I was wildly glad.

By now, Mrs Chandles was in her room resting. Many years ago she had slipped and fallen and she had got a bad leg which was still giving her trouble. Mostly, she retired about now. She was probably asleep already. I hurried up what I was doing so I could go underneath the house and think about next week-end and the Monday following. That was school-day for me.

I remained under the house quite a while, then it occurred to me that Mrs Chandles might be wanting me. I thought I would go up in a little while. It was all silence above and there was no reason to think Mrs Chandles was not asleep, but I was uneasy nevertheless.

The evening had darkened but it was not yet pitch-black, and I was sitting comfortably and looking at the dusk among these big concrete pillars. Beyond the pillars, glimmers of light came through the spaces in the fence. The place felt very still. It was as though the town were a long way away.

I sat there wondering if I should go up now. Just to see what was going on. There was a strange heady smell drifting from the front and it was from the 'Ladies of the Night', in the flower-baskets. I thought I'd better get up now, definitely, and go and see if the old lady wanted me.

I got up and frantically sat down again. There were two shadows, clear-cut, against one of the pillars. My heart pounded. They were almost in a clear line with me and at the moment I could think of no way to escape this without being seen. I did not want Mr Chandles to see me. Whatever happened I did not want him to know I was there. I eased from my seat and tried to slide behind the other face of the pillar. I was afraid to make too much movement. Perhaps that was where the perfume was coming from. Here was the Lady of the Night!

I was sure that so far I had not been seen. Whispering was coming across but it was very muffled. Then Mr Chandles' voice rose, and it was appealing and caressing and tender, and I heard him saying, 'Jule, Jule,' many times. I stood up, holding myself square against the pillar. I breathed heavily. I wanted to get away. I remained fixed behind the pillar. After a few moments I peeped to see how their heads were, and I saw that their heads were together and they were in an embrace. I dashed to the next pillar. I stood behind it, my heart racing, and I waited to see if everything remained quiet. Then I peeped again. From this position I could not see them at all. The back steps were only two pillars away. I counted one, two, three, then made a dash for the back steps.

I was so relieved to be indoors, but I was still feeling uneasy. I went quietly to the place where I slept. The drawing-room door was already shut. Mrs Chandles had retired for the night. I thought the best thing for me to do was to go to sleep right away. I wondered what would have happened if the old lady had called while I was behind the pillar down there. Jeesan Christ! I thought. I made my bed quickly and changed my clothes. Then I shut the back door and went to sleep.

ELEVEN

As the weeks passed I saw Julia quite often, though at first I could hardly look her in the face. She was so charming and pretty that I could not help but keep liking her. She asked about Mr Chandles, unashamed and one day she let me know that she was responsible for my going to Government School.

'*I* told Chandy to send you there,' she said. 'I used to teach there, you know.'

'Teach?' I said, surprised.

'O that's a great school. I used to teach the infants there.'

'Really?' I said.

'Yes, of course,' she said, 'Of course, "really". Why not?'

'I didn't know you were a teacher,' I said reproachfully.

'I used to be. That's a great school. I used to like old Soames.'

'Sir?' I said.

'I mean I used to like him, but not in *that* way.' She looked at me quaintly. 'I thought you was a *little* boy.'

'Yes,' I said, 'What I mean is, I know Mr Soames and thing.'

She laughed. I supposed it was because I said I knew Mr Soames. Perhaps it was obvious I would know Sir, since Sir was the head-master. This girl laughed at everything.

'Well how about school,' she said. 'Give me the low-down.'

I gave her. School was great. March had brought this, and the hot, hot sun, and it had brought the crop-time of the canes. For me this was the Dry Season, but here the weather was called, 'The Crop'. On mornings as I walked to school the sugar-cane fields would be white.with the mists, and in the near parts you could see the workers already chopping down the canes. All day long the cane-wagons would be set upon by gangs of children as they passed near the Government School, and I had never known sugar-cane so sweet as in these parts.

The Usine Ste Madeleine was only a few miles away, across Navet. Its three giant chimneys were always puffing smoke now, and at nights we could see the lights of the many mill-houses, and if it was quiet, we could hear how the machines crushed the canes. From the streets on evenings we watched the blazing fields. Before the cane was cut they set fire to the field to chase out the vermin, and the dry trash would make beautiful flares in the dusk. Many people came out to watch because at times it looked as if the whole country was alight. They would stand there fascinated by the fire and the crackle and then there would be talk of how hot the night was.

By then I had got to know Owen who lived nearby in our street. He would be there on such evenings and sometimes Learie, who came from further down the street would be there, too, and I would stand on the pavement with them both, talking, but listening to hear if Mrs Chandles would call. I would wish she was asleep. Usually, however, her voice would come, faint and high-pitched, 'Francis! Francis!' and I would slip away leaving my friends in the road. Mainly, she would ask me if I had watered the plants yet, and I would hurry down the steps for the watering can. By the time I came back out to the front the two boys would be gone.

The heat of the Crop Season took such a toll on the flower-plants that I had to water them every day. The crispy earth seemed to drink up the water around them. Even though I soaked these plants on evenings, the next day's sun would leave them dry and withered and sickly-looking. Mrs Chandles never believed I watered them properly, except when she came to see for herself.

Hardly anything remained green under the stinging sun. Even she herself looked withered and dry.

I had seen from the very start that she could not stand the heat. On these hot, dry afternoons she opened all the windows and went to bed. She got pains all over her body, and this was especially because of that fall, and when I came home from school my first job would be to massage her legs from knees to ankles with Sacrool, the Indian Sacred Oil. There was always a new bottle of this mystical oil about. I used a great deal of energy, rubbing the oil into those legs of hers, and she spoke of miraculous relief, but when I was finished she would seem even more exhausted than I was, and would go straight off to sleep.

Those sleepful moments were my long moments of freedom. Those were the times when I went playing in the schoolyard next door and made so many new friends. Every evening Owen used to come back to the school-yard to have games with the throngs of other boys, and joining them sometimes, I would find myself in the middle of the games and enjoying myself as if I had fully belonged to that crowd and that school.

Although my other friend Learie went to the Government School, sometimes he too came up the street to have games with the boys of Coffee R.C. When I could not go over I usually stood on our side of the fence and watched them. Learie was popular with the boys of Coffee R.C. for the reason that he had grown up with them in our street. Also when he came up from the Government School side he always came with an armful of cane he had pulled from the cane-wagons and he would have all the boys around him while he shared out joint by joint.

And so in this manner the crop-time went on, the days being dry and hot, the cane-fires reddening the dusk. Even if you were indoors, you knew the fires were there, by the burnt-sugar smell, and you could still hear the crackling, and if you looked through the window you could see the bits of burnt cane-leaves which the wind blew into the town.

TWELVE

When April came the heat was almost too much to bear. The flower-plants in the veranda seemed beyond needing water, and even the big trees about seemed bowed before the fury of the sun.

Mrs Chandles became very irritated by the weather and she opened all the windows very wide that whatever breeze there was might come into the house, and often she went to bed without letting me rub the pain away with the mystical oil. She complained that it was mainly the heat from the Usine Ste Madeleine, and from the burning cane-fields, that made the crop-time so unbearable, and she said it would be a blessing when a little rain came down.

But I was glad of this weather. For on afternoons when I returned from school, the noises of the boys playing in the school-yard next door would excite me, and Mrs Chandles' going to bed would be the chance for me to slip away.

The week would run out in this manner until Saturday, and Saturdays would be quite different because Mr Chandles was coming home. But it was not different, though, for the boys in the schoolyard. They still came and had games, and there was so much noise and laughter that they drew Mr Chandles to the window time and time again.

Mr Chandles had not changed towards me nor towards the old lady, and while he was there the atmosphere in the house would be as tense as ever, and I would stay around, yet keeping out of his way as much as I could. Now that his marriage seemed definite, Mrs Chandles had grown quite chilly towards him, and did not fuss over him as much as before. And I liked her for this and tried to please her in every way. Saturday and Sunday would go at snail's pace, and it would seem for me a long and dangerous journey to Monday morning. And Monday morning itself would bring relief and joy. I would lie in bed listening as the silence was shattered by Mr Chandles' feet on the floor. Finally the front door would be flung open and the clap-trap of those feet would be deadened by the concrete steps. Then the gate would open and he'd be gone.

Now, after these tense week-ends we relaxed and forgot Mr Chandles for a while. It being so hot these days, and so blindingly bright, I often recalled the dry season at home. There we liked it in the dry season for we could walk down the clear path behind our house and cross the stream and go down into the coconut fields and right up on the hills. On the hills it would be breezy, and looking east, there would be the coconut palms stretching away below and above them a fringe of blue sea. And here we would sit and talk and probably climb one of the coconut trees and pick waternuts to drink. Afterwards we would collect the dry fallen branches and take them home for firewood. Mostly, while wending our way back we'd pass through the guava patch to look at the lily pond. It would be so dry that even the bottom would be scorched and we would walk upon the bottom where only a few months before there was so much water. There would be no sign of the alligator that used to be here. All the lilies would be dead.

Also, I often thought of the cricket we played in the yard under the scorching sun. Ma would be over at the Forestry Office but even from there she would hear the clang of the old drum when someone was bowled and she would come rushing to the tiger-wire fence to drive us in from the heat. When she went back we would steal chances to play and not make much noise, but in the late afternoon, when the sun cooled, it would be all right, and we could play freely until it was too dark to see.

When I thought of these things my mother stood out big in my mind. She stood out bigger than everything. Sometimes she would be a little way in the background, but when I recalled how she came up to the tiger-wire, she was right in the centre of my mind.

I was longing to see her. At school we wrote letters for exercises. When I got any more spare pennies I would get writing paper and a stamp and I would write a letter to her. Many times I thought of her and remembered her vividly and was near to tears.

THIRTEEN

Holy Thursday was the first time I saw Edwin, Mrs Chandles'
other son. He came to bring Easter gifts to Mrs Chandles and when
I saw the man open the gate I had no doubt at all who he was. He
looked so much like the Mr Chandles inside, it partly terrified me.
I watched him as he came towards where I was watering the plants
and stood up.

'Hello,' he said.

I said, 'Hello.'

'Mayaro feller, eh?' he said, laughing.

'Yes,' I said.

'Nice, nice!' he said, still laughing.

It seemed easy for him to smile. He stood there a moment and I
went on self-consciously watering the plants. All the time I was
thinking how big he was and how much like, yet how very
different, from the Mr Chandles inside.

Then he said, 'Mother at the back?'

'Yes, Mr Chandles.'

'My name is Edwin,' he said.

I was silent.

'What's your name again?'

'Francis,' I said.

'Well this is Edwin here,' he said. We both laughed.

I held my breath as he walked up the steps and went into the
house. Mr Chandles had arrived at noon on that Holy Thursday
and I had not too long ago seen him in the drawing-room reading
the *Illustrated London News*. I did not know what to expect at the
encounter of these two, but nothing happened. I heard not a sound
as Edwin walked through, and I heard him call, 'Mother!'

Mrs Chandles answered from the kitchen. The voice was tremulous and excited. 'Oo!' she cried. 'Well! *You* here?'

'Yes. Right here. In the flesh!'

I put the watering can to the plants again. I was waiting as if for an explosion. However not a sound came from the Mr Chandles in the drawing-room. Edwin stayed for about an hour, talking and joking, and he walked about the house as though he lived here every day, and as if the one in the drawing-room was not here at all. Finally, he said good-bye to the old lady. He asked for me and when I came he shook hands and said cheerio. Then he walked out through the drawing-room again and went away.

For the rest of the evening I could feel the tension in the house. Mr Chandles hardly spoke but I could see the nervousness on his face. I kept away as much as I could. Mrs Chandles, too, was unusually quiet, and there was that self-satisfied look about her – a look almost of defiance. We went to bed without a word spoken in the house but the next morning the sound of angry voices woke me up.

I lay there listening. I had never heard them quarrel so fiercely before. I wondered if the neighbours were listening. Mrs Chandles sounded like the screeching of some wild bird, and Mr Chandles in his anger was loud and booming, and you could almost feel the house shake when he talked. I did not feel comfortable being in the middle of this pandemonium. I thought I'd get up and go underneath the house.

Mr Chandles was saying quite a lot of things I had not heard of before. It was clear that Edwin's arrival had nettled him, and he was so furious. I was half afraid he would be violent against the old lady. Mrs Chandles stood her ground with determination. She said why the hell didn't he squawk when Edwin was there. He said if he laid his hands on either of them it would be murder. He knew that. He said God in heaven could hear him, but if she and Edwin thought they'd have the house it would be blood and sand first.

I had already cleared out from upstairs and was underneath the house. The voices came plainly to me and I was certain the neighbours around could hear. It was Good Friday morning and most people around were rising to go to church. I felt we were a disgrace to Romaine Street.

Upstairs the voices rattled on. They seemed to have forgotten that I was around. The things they were saying astonished me. Quite a lot seemed to have happened between Mrs Chandles and her two sons and dead husband. But it was difficult to know exactly what to believe.

I knew I could not believe that Mrs Chandles had destroyed the old man. She had spoken very little of him, but when she had, she had spoken well. I felt that it was Mr Chandles' bitterness that made him say such things, and it was clear the bone of contention was the house. I remembered Edwin who had come here only yesterday, and you could see on his face that he was a gentleman, and that he meant well. He was much nicer than either of these two. I was definitely on his side, despite the terrible things Mr Chandles said about him.

I stopped thinking of Edwin to listen again. Mrs Chandles was talking of the money she had spent on their education. This was not new to me. She had always boasted about this – about the upper-class education she had given her children. Both boys had gone to the big college. I had seen the college myself, on the hill, and I had gazed upon it with awe. I had also seen Mr Chandles' coat with the college things on. And now I thought of our own poverty and of my mother sending me here because she could hardly feed us all. Yet no such row could take place in Ma's house. And we weren't refined or anything. And we had not been to the big college.

For most of the morning the quarrel died and flared up and died and flared up again. Then, as fortune would have it, Mr Chandles dressed and went out. As soon as he left and I went indoors, Mrs Chandles started glaring at me as if I was the cause of all the unrest, and I felt very uncomfortable in the house. She did not make any meals that day. For lunch she ate bread and butter and cheese and she gave no thought to my being hungry. I watched her eating, her toothless jaw opening and shutting like crab-traps, and when she was satisfied, she hobbled into her room and shut the door.

Mr Chandles had always kept tins of marie biscuits in the bottom of the safe. I had never given them a thought before, but now, being so hungry, I waited until I couldn't hear Mrs Chandles stirring in her room – which meant she was in bed – and I came into the kitchen, held one of the tins against my body so it would make very little noise on opening, and then I filled both my pockets with marie biscuits and went to the bathroom downstairs.

I saw Mrs Chandles only once more for the rest of that day. The morning's encounter must have left her exhausted. She came out and went to the veranda to look at the flower-plants, and seeing this, I dashed to the bathroom to get the watering can. I came round with the water. 'Fool!' she cried, 'You'll wet them in this steaming sun! You want to kill them or what!' I went back round with the can. From downstairs I heard the door of her room slam shut.

I did the rest of my work as usual, not forgetting to water the plants when the sun was cool. Then I sat on the back steps and I wondered to myself what sort of human being this old lady could be. She hadn't cooked. She couldn't expect that I had eaten. She had left me to starve and like Mr Chandles she did not care a damn.

I sat on the back steps for some time and I was very low in spirit. Mrs Chandles did not call and it must have been dusk before I got up.

FOURTEEN

Mr Chandles came back late that night. I wanted to tell him about the marie biscuits but I was afraid. I thought I'd leave him to find out for himself. Then I'd say I didn't know anything about them. I'd swear to God I didn't.

The next day passed without much happening. Mr Chandles remained at home for a while and then he went away and did not come back until evening. But the tense uneasy atmosphere hung over the house I tried to avoid the old lady just as much as I tried to avoid Mr Chandles, and I kept so well away that during the morning I did not notice Mrs Chandles had left my breakfast on the table. When I saw it the tea was cold and there were flies hovering about the slice of bread. There was also a thin slice of cheese. I sat down and ate.

I watched out for my lunch but it was well into the afternoon before that was ready. I ate it hungrily and was still feeling to eat. The day was Gloria Saturday but this thought hardly occurred to me. I was feeling so depressed and miserable. And now they were starving me. I did so much work but Mrs Chandles was so mean with the food. She was still angry because of Mr Chandles and she was taking it out on me. But I would not be starved once there was something to eat in the house. There were two things I would do if they didn't give me more food. Firstly, I would steal rather than go hungry, and secondly, I would write and tell Ma that I was starving and she must come quickly and take me away.

About the first plan I was unsure because I was afraid. It would be terrible if Mr Chandles found out that I was stealing. I couldn't bear to think of it. It would not be rosy for me if he found out.

The second idea, pleasant as it was, seemed hopeless to me. Ma seemed so far away she might have been in some other world. I had written and posted a letter to her but that seemed to have melted in the silence. Ma seemed as lost as she was in the dreams I had dreamed and half-forgot on waking. I was dejected and despaired.

I went and sat on the steps. That was a long dull evening that I sat in, and though the thoughts of this house depressed me greatly, the thoughts of my own home weighed me down even more. When the sun went down I watered the plants again, and the darkness fell thickly and heavily that night.

At the clearing up of the next morning Mr Chandles went away again. The old lady woke me up to send me to the market and to my surprise there was not the least bit of anger in her voice. Walking quickly, I was soon hurrying down Keat's Street. Still, the market was already buzzing with people when I got there. I had to push my way to get anywhere near the merchants. I had never seen the market packed like this. I arrived back late but Mrs Chandles was not annoyed.

There was elaborate preparation and plenty of cooking that morning, and, though it was Easter Day, I was a little surprised about this. Mrs Chandles had made me polish the dining-table till it was spotless and she had brought in one of her best anthuriums from the veranda and put it on the table. There was much stewing going on in the kitchen and the odours made me hungry in a most unbearable way.

And just before lunchtime all the preparation explained itself. Mrs Princet arrived. Mrs Princet was the most cheerful person I had seen for a long time and from the time she came into the house there was so much laughter that it made me laugh too.

She had brought things for Mrs Chandles, even a bottle of cyder, and the cyder was brought out at lunch, and I had the most unexpected honour of sitting at table with Mrs Chandles and Mrs Princet. Mrs Princet seemed to think it was a natural thing for me to be there and maybe she thought I lunched with Mrs Chandles every day, but I felt so uncomfortable and out of place sitting here that I hardly knew what I was doing. But I knew I was very glad Mrs Princet had come.

Mrs Chandles, herself, was very strange. I had never seen her so cheerful, nor so full of life. She laughed and talked and she put twice as much food on her plate as I knew she would manage to eat. She brought out glasses for drinks.

They talked about all sorts of things; about these changing times, and about the good old days that would never come back. Then Mrs Princet asked about Mr Chandles in code fashion and the old lady answered likewise, and I, looking elsewhere, pretended I could not understand. Then Mrs Princet said, 'And Lind was so sweet! Remember Mon Repos?'

'Oh, girl! You talking about donkeys years now. He was only about nine then.'

'You was a young chick then.'

'Ah, yes, yes. That's life, eh, girl?'

There was silence for a while.

Afterwards Mrs Chandles asked about Winston. Winston was a grandson who was heading for great things. Mrs Princet presently went into an account of Winston's college life and it soon became clear that he was intelligent far beyond his years. How else could he be doing *mathematics* and *science*? I felt a little jealous that such a young boy should be so promising. Mrs Chandles, appreciating these things, but not half so well as Mrs Princet, cut across the conversation.

'What about – er – you know what – he studying *that* yet?'

As she said this, she cleared her throat, and there was a suggestive smile on her face, and she looked at me once or twice to see if I looked as though I understood. Mrs Princet began laughing. Before she could answer, Mrs Chandles said, 'by the way, Francis, if you finish, you could go and have some fresh air, if you want.'

But it was obvious that Mrs Princet did not attach any secrecy to things like that. 'Girl!' she said, almost choking with laughter, 'I have a joke to give you. Oh! Oh, don't kill me!'

I went out and sat down on the back steps. I did not hear the joke about Winston but it was obvious it was about some girl. I did not blame him. Girls were there to be liked. Some of them were very beautiful. Some of them with the long plaits. And with the nice shy smiles. I liked girls.

I noticed how cool and pleasant the wind was. There were little love-birds jumping about along the top of the fence where it was all galvanized sheets, and a cat from the house just beyond our fence was in our yard, walking about stealthily and swinging its tail from side to side. I became aware that it was watching the birds. It walked up slowly to the fence then it sat down on its hind legs and tail, then it lay down in the shadow of the w.c. and looked as thought it were asleep. Then it got up and drew a little nearer to the fence. The love-birds flew away, and came back on another part of the fence.

The cat did not give up. It was trying every trick to catch the birds. But they were too smart for him. I looked at him with his big grey eyes and he looked at me and I bent to pick up a nice big stone to pelt him down with. Knowing what was coming he leaped over the fence. That sent the birds scattering wildly, cheeping.

I walked a little way past our w.c. to where the fence ended at the back of our house. The road that passed at the back of these houses was Celesta Street. The house just in front of me, and where the cat came from, obscured my view of the street, but to the right it was quite an open view because of the school-grounds which went right down to the street.

There were not many people walking by, now, though. There was not much to see, except the houses. In the heat of the day all the windows were open and some of the front doors were open too, and all the jalousies I could see, were let down. In the verandas were the rows of boxes with flower-plants in them, and I could make out anthurium lilies from here. The plants looked greener than ours but I was sure if I went near up I would see they were just as withered. I looked through the windows to see if I could distinguish persons. I could not see anybody. Under one house I could see a hammock tied to posts but it was not swinging and it did not look as if anybody was inside it. Standing here, I felt the galvanized sheets quite warm against me. The love-birds did not come near this part of the fence. Neither did the cat come back. For a while I stood looking over into Celesta Street, then I went and sat on the steps in the cool.

I was sitting on the highest step where I could just hold the view of Celesta Street. I could see the white road running up a slight incline towards the Coffee Street. I thought of how the Coffee Street had so many little streets running up and down into it, and how she herself threaded her wide way, weaving here, winding there, until she met the High Street by the Library Corner. There was a traffic island at the Library Corner, and the Point-a-Pierre road ran off to the right, the Promenade bore slightly left, and the great High Street sped downhill towards the wharf.

To think of the wharf itself was very exciting. I had been in the town so many months and I had never been to the wharf. I had been quite near to the High Street – as far as the Library Corner. I had heard that all the main groceries and stores were on the High Street, and that it was the shopping centre and the glamour street of the town. Julia promised she would take me down there on Saturday, to shop, and we would go down to the wharf. This was grand to look forward to, but it was wishful thinking. I could not see how I could be away from the house for so long. For there was no question of asking Mrs Chandles' permission. I had never heard Mrs Chandles mention Julia, but I could tell how much tiger-wire lay between them, too. I had not forgotten what Brinetta had told me. I knew I could not even dare to let Mrs Chandles know I stopped on my way from market and talked to Julia. Julia's name was best left unspoken here, for it might cause more heat than the cane fires. So things like the wharf and the gulf seemed a world away. But they were nice to think about from the back steps.

The shadows which had been short before, were noticeably longer now, and I noticed that about half the backyard was shaded and half was bright. I could not see the sun but judging from the length of the shadows I guessed it must have been about three o'clock now. Hearing voices in the school-yard I looked across quickly. There were men walking up the long banistered stairway and some were walking down with desks and benches on their shoulders. At the back of the school there was an off-the-ground projecting part of the building where the concert stage was, and the men went round there with the desks and benches and were packing them against the wall. I wondered what was going on. Those who had just brought benches went back up the stairs and on their way they met those who were coming down. Mrs Chandles called to me at this time. I went in wondering what was going on at the school.

FIFTEEN

Inside, the dining-room table was all cleared up and Mrs Chandles and Mrs Princet were now sitting in the drawing-room. The cyder bottle was on the table with the cork drawn, and there were glasses and beside them a bowl of nuts. Mrs Princet must have already made acquaintance with the cyder bottle for her eyes seemed glazed. Her eyes roved along the walls at the pictures and it was as if she had never seen them before and had never known they were so exciting. Mrs Chandles was sitting back in one of the soft chairs. She did not look merry in the manner of Mrs Princet, but she looked so relaxed and friendly and satisfied, it was a wonder to see her.

'Where you was all the time?' she said.

She poured me a big drink of cyder and I put it to my head. Mrs Princet was laughing. She said, 'Careful, Franco, careful now!' The way she said this made me laugh. She was well into the 'merry' stage, and I felt that if she only smelled more cyder she'd be drunk. But perhaps she wasn't going to have any more. Maybe that was why she had turned her glass down on the carpet in front of her, and had turned her head towards the pictures. Perhaps she could not bear to look at the bottle because she knew if she touched it again she'd be dead drunk.

I thought of all this with the glass to my head. The cyder was very strong and I could not drink it off all at once. When I was finished Mrs Chandles asked if I wanted any more and Mrs Princet exclaimed, 'No, boy!' and I said, no, I didn't want any more. Mrs Chandles could not have had any of this cyder. Else she would not have asked that!

Mrs Princet said, 'Nuts?' looking at me and pointing somewhat listlessly towards the bowl. Mrs Chandles said, 'Yes, take some nuts.' I was taking one or two in my hand, but Mrs Princet dipped both her hands into the bowl and taking up two big handfuls gave them to me. They bulged out of my pockets and I went out again to the back steps.

The taste of the cyder was still very much in my mouth. I thought it a very strong drink, but nice. Now I knew what was in those dusty, pot-bellied bottles I had seen on the higher shelves of the shops. Often I had watched them and had read the words 'WHITE-WAYS CYDER', and sometimes, 'OLD WELSH CYDER', and I had always wondered what that sort of drink tasted like. Now I knew!

I placed the nuts on the lowest step, which was on concrete, and hit them down with my palm and my palm hurt a little but the nuts cracked. And then I thought, silly, why not get a good stone. And I looked for a good, clean, big enough stone and then it was very easy to crack the nuts.

I was enjoying these nuts. They were Brazil-nuts which the shops also sold at Christmas. I sat there with the sun cooler but still bright and with the shadow of our house stretching nearer to the back fence. The sky looked open and was of vivid blue, and in places there were bits of white clouds drifting very, very slowly. Looking at the clouds they seemed to take the shape of things and of faces, and there was one very like the map Mr Guilden had drawn of our 'Island Home'. But they kept changing their shapes all the time.

My heart was light and as open as the skies in a way I had hardly known it before. This was an Easter Day beautiful in itself and beautiful because of Mrs Princet, and because of the strange kindness of Mrs Chandles. I thought I should never forget it. I must have sat there long, for the afternoon was certainly looking like evening now and the shadow of our house had long caught up with the back fence. Looking at the school shadow I saw what a large part of the school-yard it had taken up now, and I also noticed that a great pile of benches was stacked at the back of the school. No men were walking up and down the stairway now. I wondered if the inside of the school was as naked as it was born!

Seeing the sun had cooled I thought I'd better go and water the plants. I did not want to spoil the day by having Mrs Chandles after me now. I went to the bathroom for the watering-can and I made several trips with it, watering the plants very generously. Those on the front steps and those on the ground, I fairly soaked, but I was careful with the ones in the veranda, particularly those in the hanging wire-baskets, for when watering them it was easy to splash the floor below and make a mess. I took my time and wanted to do a nice job.

While I was still watering the plants my heart gave a hard thump for I heard Mrs Princet's voice at the front door. She was coming out to go. Presently she was out in the veranda and she said, 'Oh, Francis, you out here?' And she put her hand on my shoulder and said she was going and she'd see me again.

I was very touched and very full inside. Mrs Chandles was in the veranda seeing her off and Mrs Princet walked off towards the Coffee Street, and every now and again she turned back to wave, until she was out of sight. Then Mrs Chandles shook her head and said, half to me, half to herself, 'What a girl, eh? Hm! What a girl!' And I knew within myself how right she was. Mrs Chandles looked at a begonia beside her and she straightened the flower and she said I was watering the plants well. Then she went in, saying she was fagged out.

I was still feeling very light and very happy inside. Though Mrs Chandles wasn't staying to examine the plants I took my time so as to water them just right. You could put too much water just as you could put too little. You don't have to make the flower-pots into a swimming pool. Watering like that could rot the roots. You had to know how to do it. I worked with a joy so new and different that it looked as though the cyder had really gone to my head.

The evening was dying now. The sun must have been low over the gulf. I could see the western sky blood-red over the houses, as if the evening was being slain, and was bleeding out. It was a sombre thought, but there was also the feeling of splendour in the evening light, and the feeling of happiness and of things being good. I was thrilled. This seemed the end of a perfect day.

SIXTEEN

This feeling remained for a long time. After the plants were watered I went in again through the back steps, and there was something for me to eat on the dining-room table. Mrs Chandles was already in bed. I imagined her already in deep sleep – for the very little things put a strain on her, and today had been a big day. At best, she could not remain on her feet long. Despite the magical powers which she, and the makers, claimed for the Indian Sacred

Oil, she could not turn about much in the kitchen without having to hobble to a chair in pain. Of course, she would get up again after a while and appear refreshed, but her lameness always had the better of her.

Today she had not moved about a lot but she had talked and laughed heartily and I knew what such laughter did to her. In rare moments I had succeeded in drawing convulsive laughter from her. Funny things happened at school and also on the way to and from school and very little escaped me. I selected the funniest of these, mostly the scandalous ones, and pretending I could not unravel them myself, I told them to her. She would look at me curiously at first and I would look as innocent as possible. Then she would burst out laughing, almost hysterically, because of what I had said and because I did not know what it was really about – but in the middle of her laughter she would hold her belly and sink into the nearest chair, grimacing with pain. Afterwards she would look at me bitterly, as if I had deliberately told her such things that this would happen to her.

So I was not surprised that she was laid up now. It could not be half-past six yet. Normally I would have welcomed her going to bed because I never felt comfortable when she or Mr Chandles was about – although for short moments she could be very nice. Today, as a whole, she was so pleasant to me. Thinking of this I felt greatly encouraged. Yet I doubted she would remain so. It was far too good to hope for. Besides, it was quite clear that it was Mrs Princet that had caused the difference. I remembered what their meeting was like, today. Mrs Chandles had been so overjoyed she did not know what to do. I had never seen her so child-like before. That was a very strange moment. They were such different people and yet they were such great friends.

I got up from the dining-room and went into the kitchen. Outside it was pitch-black now. In the crop-time, more than ever, night fell suddenly. One moment the evening was bleeding and the next moment it died. I did not put on the kitchen lights but went to the window and looked out. The night was full of sounds, and before me, people were walking by on Celesta Street.

After standing there a little while my mind went back to the school on the next side. It was there that some of the noises were coming from. I leaned as far out of the window as was possible and looked, but I could see only the end part of the school. But there was light on different parts of the school-yard. The light came

55

from pressure-lamps that must have been just hung up, for the patches of light were moving to and fro, looking very weird against the darkness.

I went down into the yard. The school was indeed flooded with light and through the open windows I could see at least two lamps, so bright they hurt the eye. I wasn't surprised about the pressure-lamps because I had known there was no electric lighting in the school. They never used lights in schools, anyhow.

I was getting quite interested in what was going on at the school. Through the windows I could see the heads of people moving about. Of course I knew what was developing. They were holding a dance.

Standing right up to the fence I tried to see as much as I could. There was not much I could see because the windows were too high. I had to content myself looking at the shadowy heads moving in all directions. Some passed with chairs held high and there was one with a long, gleaming case. They seemed anxious to get the place ready. Every now and again laughter rang out in the night.

I wondered how long would it be before the dance started. Mr Chandles came to mind. He might come in late as well as he might come in earlier than I expected. If he came and I wasn't in the house that would be something! I had to keep my ears busy while I was standing here. If I heard the gate open, or footsteps in the house, I'd just dash inside. I hoped Mr Chandles would stay away as long as he'd stayed on the other nights. If he did I could remain until the music struck up and perhaps I could then bring the soap-box from under the house and stand on it and watch people dancing.

There were many little things that came to view as I strained to see through the school windows. In one corner a few people were trying to hang up a lamp. I could see the heads of those standing on the floor and then there was the full body of a man holding a pressure-lamp. He must have been standing on a chair. His back was turned to me and I could only make out he had a dark suit on. He stretched high with the lamp and then the lamp was hanging there. It looked as if the lamp was hanging in space. And then there wasn't the man any more but only the sea of heads below. And the ground moved from view.

I went on thinking of the pressure-lamp in a sort of way. In the town there was still a number of houses with lamps but by far the majority of houses had electricity. Our house had electricity. There

56

was electric street-lighting also and some streets were lit up all through the night.

There was no such thing as electricity at Mayaro. Not a single house had that. And as for pressure-lamps, only two houses had this – the Forestry Office, and the doctor's home. You could see the doctor and Mrs Samuels were proud about this and they felt they were very modern. And they were, too, considering.

Things seemed to be taking such a long time to get ready in the school. But more people had come now and there were heads everywhere. I wondered if I should go for the soapbox. I noticed there were voices coming from the street now in front the school. Perhaps the dance crowd was gathering. I thought it would be a good idea to go out at the front and see. I need not stay long if I went out at the front. Out there I would be able to see fully inside the school, through the front door. There may be lots of people coming to the dance. I was getting excited. I could just go out there and stay a few minutes and come back to the fence.

I looked up to the glass window of Mrs Chandles' room. It was in darkness, as I expected. Mrs Chandles must have been snoring away by now. I thought again, Should I chance it? And I thought, Why not? It would be all right.

Under the house it was pitch-black. Only a tiny streak of light escaped through the fence from the school-yard. It ran weirdly under the house ending right up on a concrete pillar. I thought, if I was going I'd better go now, right away, and not waste any more time. The talking in the road was quite distinct and it made me feel cheerful. I took a last glance at Mrs Chandles' window and then I hurried into the darkness among the pillars.

The next moment I started back, my heart thumping. My head was all hot and wild. On getting into the back yard again I ran straight up the steps and into the house. I was confused and weak from the shock. I had run almost right into them. You couldn't miss the perfume and you couldn't mistake Mr Chandles even in the dark. I fixed up my bed without turning on the light and lay down.

My heart was thumping. This time they certainly knew I saw them. They had straightened up against the wall, and I was so near I could have touched them. I wondered what was going to happen next. I wondered what would happen when Mr Chandles came inside. It was not my fault that I had seen them. I tried to think of something to say if Mr Chandles asked me anything. I wouldn't know how to look up into his face. For he knew it was bound to be me who had appeared in the darkness. It couldn't have been anybody else. If he asked me what I'd been doing out there I'd say I'd forgotten the watering-can at the front. But perhaps he might do something without asking anything. I should not have gone out to the front! I should not have seen him there with Julia! I had no excuse. We had nearly collided. It was so dark I could have hardly seen the concrete pillar. They had been kissing.

I wiped the perspiration round my head with my sleeves. I was feeling desperate. I thought, Why couldn't he take Julia elsewhere so I wouldn't keep coming upon them? I was still trembling with fear. I kept on feeling desperate and then I began trying to calm myself and I said, 'The hell with Julia!' And then I began wondering if Mr Chandles would come in any minute now. I wondered if he would come straight to me and ask me something. I would say I had forgotten the watering-can at the front. I wondered if he would come and be in a temper right away.

I was still trying to be calm and to forget if Mr Chandles would come up to have a word with me. In a strange way Julia kept weighing on my mind. I passed my sleeves all round my head again and now they were wet. Blasts of music started coming from the school. I could hardly think of them but I could hear them coming short and sharp, seeming to stab the air. I could hear the low hum of voices in that outer darkness. The blasts stopped. The hum of voices seemed raised now. The first set struck up.

Stardust, they were playing. I liked it but now I did not think of it much. I lay with my heart racing, waiting for Mr Chandles' footsteps, and at the same time I could not help thinking what a dog Julia was. I turned from one side to the other and I felt as if there was a heat on my face. I said to myself, 'She pretty but she's only a tramp!' I turned and removed the wet bedclothes from under my cheek. And I lay in pain for some time.

SEVENTEEN

Easter was almost forgotten when I had the biggest surprise of my life. I had just returned from the market and was going up to the Coffee Street, when I saw my mother coming along the pavement. 'Ma,' I cried, running towards her. I absolutely forgot myself.

I held on to her, almost delirious with joy. She squeezed me to her, her hands on my head. I said things and my words just seemed to spurt out and I did not quite know what I was saying. I held on to her in the road and would not let her go. The way she talked – her very voice – made me not want to look up into her face. After a little time I looked up. She, too, had been overcome. She had a big handkerchief mopping her eyes, and seeing me look up she hastily blew her nose and looked away. But her eyes filled up again.

'It's over there,' I said, showing the Chandles' house.

She looked at the house in a bewildered way as if she was seeing and did not understand. She was looking at everything in that manner. Her eyes caught the school, and then went back to the house I had shown. She was standing well on the side of the pavement now because a car had sped down Romaine Street. There were not many things turning down Romaine Street, but she looked very carefully up along it, then down, and we crossed the street quickly. She hesitated before the house and I pushed the gate open.

Ma must have felt fulfilled to look upon Mr Chandles' house. Even I, now so well used to it, was always impressed whenever I looked upon it from the street. There was no denying but that it was one of the finest houses of the town. You had to admit that.

And yet Ma did not seem excited to watch. In fact she was looking at it now and not appearing to take any particular notice of it. She looked at everything but her eyes seemed giddy and wandering. I left her on the steps and dashed to the back to tell Mrs Chandles Ma had come.

Mrs Chandles in her hobbling way, hurried out to the front

door. She tried to put little things right before opening the door and in her haste she knocked down a few things to the floor. Then quickly she went back to her room and came out with a vase of imitation flowers. I slid past her and went out to Ma, bringing her in by the hands.

'Well, well, well!' Mrs Chandles said, her eyes shining, her smile toothless and very wide.

'Well Mrs Chandles,' Ma said, 'I live to see the day.'

I watched their greetings and their embrace and I was very touched. I was overjoyed that Mrs Chandles should receive Ma so warmly. Apart from the way she had welcomed Mrs Princet here, I had never seen her make so much of anyone.

She called Ma, 'Francis' mother' most of the time, and they got into easy talking. And then I remembered I had been going to the shops. I took up the basket and skipped out.

I did not go to school that day. Mrs Chandles was amused to see how excited I was. Ma couldn't take her eyes off me. She was saying to Mrs Chandles how I had grown. Hoping to impress Ma I went about my work as usual, although there was no need to. I could have just stood around doing nothing. I listened to them talking. I was anxious to be alone with Ma, to ask her lots of things. Perhaps we could go somewhere – anywhere, us two alone, and we would watch the town a little, and she would even see how well I understood the town, because I had spent many months here. But Mrs Chandles talked and talked and there seemed to be no work at all getting done. And thinking of work, then, I remembered I had not yet watered the flower-plants.

Because the days had grown so blistering hot I watered the plants both morning and evening now. The sun was not too high and I thought I'd better water them before it got too hot for that. And before Mrs Chandles found out, too. For she was sure to show her plants to Ma. They were her pride and joy. I wouldn't have liked her to find them dry because this was not the morning for her to find fault with me. My head was feeling excited as I brought can after can of water to the front. I could hear Ma and Mrs Chandles talking in the drawing-room. I couldn't hear what they were saying. I held the can low over the plants in the yard and I watered them generously, letting the water run down to the roots and soak in. Then I watered those on the steps, without splashing the steps too much, and afterwards I started on the veranda ones, doing those in the wire-baskets first.

While I was still watering the wire-basket plants I heard the drawing-room door open, and then looking down I saw Ma in the veranda. I was standing on the veranda rails to reach the baskets and she looked scared about my being so high. 'Mind,' she said. 'Careful!'

'It's orright,' I said.

I was delighted that it looked dangerous for I wanted her to see that I was also brave, that I could do things. But she didn't seem to feel proud about that. Then she came right up under me and looking up into my face her mouth was more action than words.

'How they treating you?'

'Good,' I said.

Her eyes looked large and seemed to be forming tears again at the corners. I noticed that her face was a little more sunken, so her cheek-bones stood out. Her head, very full of hair, surprised me because I had not remembered so much grey upon it. Looking at her like that from right above her, and seeing her eyes looking so full of pain, I at once felt weak and desolate. I felt there must be some trouble at home. Else why was her hair so grey and why were her cheeks sunken so?

'What's wrong, Ma?' I said. 'Any trouble?'

'No. Only you.'

'I okay here,' I said.

'You ain't get fat at all.'

I turned away. Ma's eyes were getting watery and I did not want to see her cry again. I didn't get fat but I did not know why I should get fat even if they were treating me good. I wanted to ask about Sil and Anna and Felix but I couldn't do so with Ma like this. I rested the can on the plant ledge and hopped down on to the veranda floor.

She was going to say something again and I felt uneasy because I did not want to whisper here in the veranda. When you weren't seeing Mrs Chandles you could never tell where she was. Sometimes you heard her coming up and at other times you did not hear a thing but she was there. I wanted to talk now of things which I could say loudly and perhaps during the day we would get a chance to be alone and we'd talk of other things.

'What time you left home?' I said.

'First bus. Five o'clock this morning. God, this place far!'

This place was far. I remembered that evening when we seemed to have spent ages on the bus. I wondered who was driving this morning.

'Who was driving, Edgill?'

'No, Dorwin.'

'We came down with Edgill and Balgobin.'

'Yes, Balgobin say you was shy for him.'

'I wasn't shy for anybody!' I laughed.

'He is a nice boy,' she said.

'Yes.'

Balgobin, in truth, was the best fellow I knew. He was vulgar and coarse but I liked him.

'What about Anna?' I said.

'Oh she's there. She went up to sixth. Time for her to leave school, though, and learn some sewing.'

Ma was always saying that. Next year Anna would be in seventh. There would be no higher class for her to go to. I suppose she'd have to go somewhere next year. Perhaps learning to sew was the best thing. Perhaps.

Ma always had some plan for the future. She spoke now of Felix getting a job at St Joseph factory when he left school. Cyril, the foreman, had promised that. He liked Felix because when we played cricket down in the savannah sometimes Felix could bat very good. Cyril lived in the house just on the edge of the savannah and every evening he sat in front the house with his hands under his chin and looked at the cricket in the savannah. He didn't talk much but he knew all who were very good. He had called Felix once and told him he was very good. And he had told Felix to keep it up and that he would get a job to work under him at the estate. It would be a little while before Felix left school but Ma was counting on this job. She always counted on things far away. She counted on Anna getting married, and on Sil taking up teaching, and she counted on having life easy one of these days. This gave her much strength.

She came up near to me again and I knew she was going to whisper something. She looked around at the door and she said softly, if I was getting bad treatment here I'd better say right now because she did not know when she'd be here again. I said everything was all right. I looked at the door uneasily and at the bedroom window that opened on the veranda and I did not want to talk about that sort of thing now. There wasn't anyone at the door or the window. That window was of Mr Chandles' room but the old lady went into it sometimes. I wondered if when I got the chance I should tell Ma of Mr Chandles and his mother. I knew Ma was under the impression they lived beautiful lives. I would laugh to see Ma's face when I told her. I wondered if I should.

I asked her about Sil and Felix and Anna again just to keep her from asking me the questions I knew she wanted to ask. She was looking at my clothes, so I knew what she wanted to find out. I diverted her conversation to the new classes Sil and Felix had gone to, for they had been sent up also. She was depressed, as always, about the number of new school-books she had to buy.

I tried to get all the latest news. She talked about home and about the folk at the Forestry Office and about the people who had passed away. Just two old-timers had passed away and there was not much change. When she was going to talk about the Forestry Office she put her hands to her mouth. She always did that when she was going to say something important. She said she had got the letter. She had taken it to the Forestry Office, and when Marva and Mrs Samuels heard it was from me, they had been all over her, congratulating her. They had said, look, I had learnt to write letters already! In just a few months!

I could see Ma was thrilled by what they said, but I wasn't. I only wanted to say I hoped Mr Chandles did not know of the letter. I was sure he wouldn't approve my writing home. But I realized that since Marva knew, it was a waste of time saying this. For I was sure he'd heard about it by now. Ma had seen him up there sometimes. He always told her I was well and happy.

I thought of telling Ma about Julia but I changed my mind. There was no point to it and the story was too complicated. I thought I'd tell her of Mrs Princet, though, when we were together and I could talk freely.

I was finished watering the plants now. I stood there and I watched my mother again to see how much she had changed and I asked her again, was everything at home all right. Her thoughts seemed far away. She said, yes, yes, just as usual, you know. I had to go to the back of the house with the watering-can. Ma went in again through the front door. As I turned to go down the steps I heard a faint creak as of the jalousie. I glanced round quickly. I saw movement in Mr Chandles' bedroom. Christ! I thought. I went round with the can trying to think of exactly what words Ma and I had said. And I wondered how long had that blinking Mrs Chandles been listening to us.

EIGHTEEN

I did not tell my mother about the eaves-dropping. She seemed to have taken to Mrs Chandles and she seemed so happy I did not want to upset her. In any case, since Easter, Mrs Chandles had been fairly cheerful with me, and now, with Ma actually finding me, so that I knew I was not lost to her, I felt much more content to stay here.

I went through the day doing my tasks busily and with a zeal that came from inside. I was very happy and proud. I was proud for Mrs Chandles to see I was not an orphan and alone. Also, that my mother was somebody she could talk with. I did all that I had to do, with the day wearing on, and in the afternoon, after lunch, we all sat together in the drawing-room. I was surprised to be there but I was beginning to feel frustrated because I wanted to be alone with Ma. I had not asked her half the things I wanted to ask her. She was chattering away with Mrs Chandles. I was surprised and a little jealous. You'd have thought Ma preferred Mrs Chandles to *me*, the way she was chattering! I was fuming cross.

When the evening set in Ma was ready to go. She was paying all attention to me now, and her eyes were getting watery again, and I knew that all the time she had been such a chatterbox in the drawing-room it was me she really loved. She had been making herself charming for my sake. I knew that. Now she was returning and I did not know when she'd come again. I was beginning to feel soft and over-full inside. I went down to the bathroom. I burst into tears before I could get inside.

I walked with Ma to the bus-stop. She said, were they really treating me good. I said yes. She was silent. Then she asked me where was the new clothes Mr Chandles had said he'd buy. She looked very troubled. I said they were in the grip. She said she had wanted to look through the grip herself and she didn't know why she didn't.

The distressed look on her face slowly went away but I had the

64

disturbing feeling that it was futile to try to hide anything from Ma. I had the feeling that she knew everything. I felt she had a good idea as to how I was faring here, and I felt she knew Mr Chandles had bought me no clothes at all.

We walked up the road talking. She said she would like to come to see me again. She put her hand on my shoulder and we walked in silence for some time. When we got out on the Coffee Street there was a bus at the bus-stop. We half-ran to the bus-stop and the driver, seeing us, waited a bit. The conductor helped with the grip and Ma went inside. The bus rolled off.

As I walked slowly back to the house I felt as though I might have been dreaming. So much had happened. And so quickly. And the day was finished now. I remembered the day Mrs Samuels had called Ma the salt of the earth.

Ma was a little thinner now, I believed, and I had seen she was much greyer and maybe there was more trouble than she had said. Maybe there were things she would not speak of. Perhaps nothing really serious. Probably just the hardship of providing for four; and of course I knew there was the trouble of maintaining the old house which grew more ramshackle every year. And yet I did not know how she kept such a brave spirit in spite of everything.

I thought of the bus speeding away and I walked slowly back to the house. The pavement along Romaine Street rose very prominently from the road and I was just slightly eased of my sadness and I stepped up on to the pavement then down to the pitch again and I walked right down the street like that. In the little spaces between the houses I could see red flickers. They were 'burning-out' – the estate people were. I stood up to watch the fire whenever I came to a little space, and I could hear the crackle and the way the flames roared in the wind. This was the last of the cane-fires, for the crop was nearly ended. Watching the fires had been a great attraction for me through all these months. They had started from far away in that great expanse of green. Now the fires were blazing out the last patch, near the town. I stood up at the big gap between the school and our house, and the fire I could see here stretched over some distance, and the flame-tongues licked the air, and they reddened a large part of the sky between the houses. Away over the brown open field I could see the dusk coming.

I stood up for a while looking at the cane-fire and at the dusk but my mind was wandering and I was thinking of the speeding bus. I wondered how far was she now. I tried to think of sugar-cane. Tomorrow the cutters would come with their cutlasses, and the field, having been scorched of vermin and needless leaves, would be quickly cut down. The mills at the Usine Ste Madeleine would still be grinding, and the three chimneys would still be puffing smoke, but really, the crop would be over. Tomorrow when I got home from school I would see brown earth where the last patch of green used to be. And perhaps the ploughs would come to this little part soon. I had often seen them working in the parts already cleared. Owen, my friend, who had been to all places, said the ploughs made long mounds and furrows as they went along. He said their work was to turn up the earth and to manure it and then the whole place was left alone until planting time. I did not know about all this. I could not see the mounds from here, nor the manure which the ploughs put on. But I had seen the planting at the beginning of the year, and then what looked like endless green fields, and lately, the fires every night. And with the fires, the three chimneys of the Usine Ste Madeleine had started puffing smoke. For they were grinding the cane. When Owen explained it, it seemed very simple for him. But for me there was always a little mystery about the cane.

I left off looking at the fires and I went home again. The thoughts of the cane had held off the feeling of dejection. Now I felt it coming like a storm.

I went indoors passing first underneath the house and up by the back steps. Mrs Chandles was probably gone to bed. I knew her legs would give up now, after this busy day.

I reckoned it must have been coming on to seven o'clock. I was too lazy to go and see the time. Anyway it couldn't be seven yet. Before I fell asleep tonight Ma would be in Mayaro. Before this very day was past she would be talking to Felix and Anna and Sil and she would be telling them what I had said to her, and what she knew to be true, and she would be a long time over this.

Then she would be telling them of the strange town with the big sugar-loaf hill in the middle, and of the traffic-laden streets and of the houses with verandas like the Forestry Office and with electric lights. They would be standing round her this very night and hearing of this. So, really, although many miles came between, it was only a part of one day that separated me from home! Sometimes I suffered so much for the want of being in that old place and for the want of seeing Felix and Anna and Sil, but it was only a very long

66

drive that kept me away from them. My eyes looked out on Celesta Street but it was not the lit-up panes I was seeing now. Dejection swept upon me. Now at this hour I was suffering for the need of home. Now I felt a prisoner in this giddy town. My heart was burning for home. For a moment I felt like crying out, but at the moment of greatest pain my mother's voice came back to me. It was as if she was here and talking. She had said, Stay and take in education, boy. Take it in. That's the main thing.

That was about the last thing she had said to me. I heard it now as plain as ever.

NINETEEN

After some time I felt as though my feet were catching cramp. I must have stood ages at the kitchen window. There was no reflection of light now above the houses or at the sides. Maybe the cane-fires had died down. Or maybe they had been put out.

I shook my feet to get rid of the cramp and I wondered how late it was now. It must be quite near to bedtime, I thought. Tomorrow it would be school again. The boys would ask me where I was yesterday and I would say my mother had come to see me. I was anxious to go to school just for that.

I was conscious now of being hungry. My belly felt hollow. The supper Mrs Chandles had left for me was chocolate tea with four slices of Holsum bread and a thick slice of cheese. I tasted the tea and put the cup back in the saucer. Chocolate tea was no good when you did not feel like it, especially when it was cold. I did not feel like eating bread and cheese either, although my belly felt hollow inside. It was strange when you were hungry and did not want to eat. My mind was far away, and then I thought I heard a sound and a moment later I jerked my mind back to the present and sat up, listening for footsteps. It was the dragging sound I had heard and I knew Mrs Chandles was up and feeling for her slippers. Now the bedroom door opened. Mrs Chandles came into the dining-room in one of her ancient night gowns.

'So you Ma gone?' she said.

'Yes,' I said.

'She get a quick bus?'

'Yes, right away.'

'That's lucky,' she said. 'You know you Ma is a nice lady, you know.'

I did not say anything, but I felt good. I knew Mrs Chandles meant this. She was not just being nice. She looked about her as if she had only come out to see if everything was all right. Then she said casually, 'I didn't know you used to write you Ma.'

My heart started beating fast. So Ma had talked about that! Or did Mrs Chandles get this while eaves-dropping?

'I wrote to Ma *once*,' I said.

'That's good. You must write.'

I didn't say anything.

'Anyway you mother's very nice, man. How long you here now?' she said, 'Let me see – this is June – you here six months now. What! Six months already! You is nearly a San Fernando boy now!'

I looked up at her broad, toothless grin and I tried to look pleasant. The fact was, I did feel a little pleasant to hear her say that. There was nothing false in her grin. On her night gown was a little brooch Ma had left with her. Right away I tried to count how many brooches my mother had left with people. There was the one Tanty Alice had. I could not think of the others straight away. This one looked odd on a night gown. A brooch on a night gown! It nearly made me laugh. Mrs Chandles thought I was smiling with her. She looked strangely pleased. Her smile had big pleats on the cheeks and under the chin and the flabby skin round her eyes were now a thousand tiny folds. Her gums showed pink and I could see the sockets and her eyes shone out like two jumbie-beads. It was strange, because she looked spooky somehow, and yet she looked so sincere, I believed in her. We smiled broadly.

TWENTY

For the rest of that week on coming from the market I passed through the Cascade Street short-cut again. After what I had witnessed that Easter night I had decided never to talk to Julia any more, so instead of coming along de Berrio Street and into the little track which brought me opposite Julia's house, I used to go into the Coffee Street, and walk along till I came to Romaine Street. I could not help glancing into Cascade Street as I passed it at the top, but I could not see into Julia's veranda because of houses blocking the view.

I had gone on thinking of Julia. She had lots of books in her book-case and despite everything I would have liked to borrow some from her. Not that she had better books. Just that I would have felt so happy to borrow the books from *her* book-case. I liked her most of all to look at her. And I liked her, too, for the sort of things she said. It didn't appear that she read the books but she always said something about them that would make her – not them – remain in my thoughts. Julia was a big girl but I had grown to want to see her always and to talk with her.

So this, together with Ma's visit, made me feel I must see Julia soon. I had not seen her for a long time and that space seemed like years. Mr Chandles still came every week-end and at those times I still kept away from him as well as away from under the house. He had never said anything to me about that Easter night but I was convinced he had seen me and I knew he must not find me there again. I remembered that after that time I had seethed with hate for Julia, but now that Ma had come and gone, and since it was Julia who had encouraged me to write, I wanted very much to tell her Ma had come. So I started passing along the old way again. And my heart thumped every time I came into Cascade Street. And it was only a matter of days before I saw her.

She had spotted me just as I entered from the track and she stood up in the veranda, both hands on her hips. I pretended not to see her because I was so glad and I was embarrassed. I looked away towards the Coffee Street and I hurried to the other side as if I was very late. My whole self was tense and anxious, waiting for Julia's voice. But it did not come. I went home with tumult in my mind, wondering all sorts of things.

I did not see her the next morning, nor the next, nor the one after that, but some time towards the end of that week she was in the veranda again. She spotted me at about the same place she did before. She just put her arms akimbo again and stood there watching. What I had thought was right. She was vexed with me and would not call to me. I wondered what had I done that she was vexed with me. I wondered what had I done!

Crossing the street I glanced towards the veranda. A car was speeding down Cascade Street. I had to move out of the way quickly and the car whizzed by. I looked to see if Julia had seen this. She stood there looking a little amused.

'Julia,' I said.

'When you want to get knocked down go in Romaine Street.'

I laughed and felt very relieved inside.

'Didn't see it coming,' I said.

'No? You didn't see it? You must be good to eat, boy.'

I laughed. Julia was laughing too but you could see she was trying not to laugh.

She said, 'I don't really mind, but it's the mess you'd make on Cascade Street, that's what I'm worrying about.' And with that she burst out laughing.

And right then I knew that all the unpleasantness had burst away too. Julia was no longer angry with me. I could see that she was glad to make fun with me and to talk to me again.

I looked at her. During the height of the crop, when the sun was really blistering, I had noticed how the faces of people looked tired and spent from the heart. Even at this time it was so and it seemed that everybody had grown years older. It was as if the sun had sapped all the life from them. But Julia was a sharp contrast. She looked even fresher and younger than I had known her, and she seemed as playful as the girls at school. Her head of full, black hair was just plaited long now, and although I had never seen her like this she looked more beautiful than ever. Her eyelashes looked thicker and blacker and they seemed so long that I wondered if she had done anything to them. I didn't think she used make-up. I had never seen lip-stick on her mouth, for one thing, nor rouge on her cheeks. She herself had talked about women with make-up. She hated them. To me some of these ladies looked all right, but even so, none – not one of them looked as pretty as she.

I said Ma had come and I watched her to see how surprised she would be. She was just staring at me calmly, the full mouth pouched a little, the lips pressed together. I wondered if she didn't hear what I said. Her eyes, large and mild, were looking at me. It was as if I hadn't said anything at all.

'Really,' I said, 'Ma came.'

She seemed to think a little, and then she said, 'I know all about that.'

'How come?'

Mrs Chandles never spoke to Julia. In any case Mrs Chandles never left the house. And it wasn't week-end yet. I couldn't understand this.

'I know all about it,' she said, 'Your Ma is Marva's friend – not true?'

I was astonished. I didn't even know she knew of Marva. And I didn't see how Marva was connected with this.

'Why Marva?'

'All right, skip it,' she said, 'You took your mother anywhere nice?'

'We didn't go anywhere. She was working all the time.'

'Working?'

'Well, helping Mrs Chandles.'

'Which one. Which Mrs Chandles?' she said, laughing meaningfully.

It was a little while before I saw what she meant. Oh, I thought, She knows about that, too! And I said to myself – jealousy! She was still looking at me.

'Who told you about Marva?'

'Who you expect?'

'How you knew Ma came?'

'I knew even *before* she came. You wrote to her. Marva is your mother's friend – not so? Well she was so proud of the letter, well she told Chandy – what you expect?'

'O God!'

'O God about what?'

I just stared into space. So that was it. Marva had told Mr Chandles. Ma had said Marva read the letter. I was stupid not to have realized Mr Chandles knew.

'He said anything?'

'Why? If you wrote your mother that's your business. But I'm telling you, watch out for this Marva, because if you slip, you slide.'

'She's nice,' I said, pretending I didn't fear her.

'She'll be nicer when she keeps her trap shut. I don't see why she had to tell Chandles about the letter.'

'Still, I didn't say anything risky.'

'That Marva!' she said cuttingly, 'Anyway that's your own people. I'd better shut up.'

'I only know her so. In the Forestry Office and thing. Mr Chandles told you about her?' I could hardly believe this.

'Chandles does tell me *everything*.'

This was the first time Julia had been so frank on this. It seemed as if she meant that between us now this part of her life must be understood. I did not feel badly about it somehow. I was so glad to be speaking to her again. I would have welcomed anything just to keep on good terms with her.

'*I know,*' Julia went on. 'Don't think I don't know. I know all about Mayaro and Marva and all that bacchanal.'

As she said this I could see she was getting worked up. Her eyes were fiery and she looked as though she would take me to task. She inclined her head to one side and said, 'Think I don't know about that so-and-so? She is his woman. *I know.*'

I did not say anything. I wished Julia wouldn't talk about this. What she said was true but I had nothing to do with it. I had never thought about that a great deal. But I had seen Mr Chandles with Marva at Mayaro and she was his woman because he had his arms about her, and besides we all knew at home they were engaged and going to get married. But I did not want to say anything. Because if I said that, Julia would get more heated. I knew she was jealous and I knew that was why she was getting in a temper. She did not seem to want to hide it that she was jealous. I was embarrassed. I told her I did not know about it. She said what exactly didn't I know about. I hushed up. She said if Marva had got me into trouble with the letter I would have known about it then. I said, 'Listen, Julia, this has nothing to do with me – why take it out on me?' She calmed down then. She was still vexed, but her manner changed. She said, 'Anyway be careful with that man.' She said, 'Be careful, because he's a very funny man.' I said I knew. She said she's telling me so don't blame her if anything happened to me.

I wanted to say *she* must be careful too. For Julia was simple and delicate and I knew Mr Chandles was very hard. Somehow I had the feeling that he could hurt her. I had the feeling that he could hurt her badly and send her away. Maybe it was good for her to be hurt, for what she was doing, but I couldn't stand her being hurt. She was simple and very delicate and although she was older than me and she had been teaching and she had a lot of fine talk I knew there was not much to her. I had the creeping feeling that one day when Mr Chandles was with her he would hurt her badly and maybe he would send her away. She looked beautiful now in the way her hair was done up and in her nice home dress. She seemed to have calmed right down. She talked about other things and I was relieved. She said every morning she had seen me pass along the Coffee Street when I wasn't talking to her. I wanted to laugh out. I said was it true she had seen me. She said yes, but only once or twice. This upset me because at first she had said she had seen me every morning. If she had seen me every morning it meant she had looked out for me. She had not, but had seen me once or twice, maybe by accident. I felt like saying Marva was Mr Chandles' girl, just to upset her. She didn't disguise that she loved Mr Chandles. And that she hated Marva. And now she didn't like Ma because Ma was Marva's friend. Julia was simple and delicate and yet she was complicated. I liked her most when she was simple. But she was very wicked, herself. Brinetta had called her a pepper-pot. It was true. I talked to her a little but I was thinking of all these things and I stood there with one foot on the step and the other on the concrete base. Then I looked away and wouldn't talk any more.

'What's wrong with you now?'

'Nothing,' I mumbled.

'Well don't worry about anything. Especially that stupid letter – I don't mean your letter was stupid. But don't worry about it.'

'No.'

'And don't worry about me and Chandles. That is big people's business.'

She looked so pompous saying this that I stared straight into her eyes. 'Who's worrying about that. I'm not worrying about that!'

'Oh, no? Well I'm only telling you.'

There was a silent moment and then I said, 'I have to go now.'

'Okay then. Cheerio. See you.'

'See you.'

I had suddenly become conscious of the length of time I had stayed. I ran all the way home now. I wondered what would I tell Mrs Chandles this morning.

TWENTY-ONE

A few weeks afterwards the weather started changing. The evenings were hot without any wind, and the sky which had been blue and speckless for months, started showing clouds here and there. The first clouds were small white ones, then they seemed to group up and form bigger ones, then there were really big ones, and these seemed low, and they were very cumbersome moving across the sky. The sunsets, usually blood-red, were not so tinted now, and when the light fell off behind the houses the day took on a dull metallic look. People noticed this and said the weather was changing.

The cane-lands had been left alone since after the ploughing and from the window thay looked dreary and empty, with the earth black, and one day Mrs Chandles said they were letting the soil rest for the next season. Mrs Chandles was much milder now. She spoke to me without anger, and on occasions she was even jovial with me. The hotness of the afternoons seemed to trouble her a great deal, and she seemed strangely grateful just because I was willing to rub away the pain with the Indian Sacred Oil. Indeed, she felt the relief that came afterwards was not only because of the oil but also because of my willing mind, and some evenings while I rubbed away the pain she spoke of this. She connected willingness of mind with sacredness and she used the words 'spiritual' and 'body' in a very confusing way. But I was glad that she conversed with me and I tried to rub down the legs very good. At times when I was finished she got upon her feet testing how they were, and mostly they would be fine and she would be cheerful and walk out into the kitchen and she would say I was a good liniment boy. Evening upon evening we stood in the kitchen looking towards the cane-lands, and though they were only vast and open she would say, 'I think the tractors manuring now, you know.' But there were no tractors in the place.

Mrs Chandles was cheerful mainly because the crop-time was finished. When the crop finished it was usually the end of the hot season. That was the reason she was so cheerful. Often, in the evenings, when the long ringing cries of the cigala would come through the window, she would stop whatever she was doing and she would say, 'Sh! Sh!' even if I wasn't making any noise at all, and we both would listen until the long whistle died away. This brought a good frame of mind to the old lady and she would go to the window and look out to see what the clouds were doing. The place would be very hot, but hearing the cigala, even I knew that the rains were close.

These weeks were very bad for the flower-plants. The end-of-crop sun seemed to carry the destroying fire. I could not understand how the plants were scorched like that. On coming from school in the evenings I would notice how all of them were withered and frizzled up. And those in the flower-pots had the earth around them cracked with the heat. I would watch, particularly, the anthuriums, for their thick leaves drooped right down as if they had lost hope, and so did the begonia leaves, for begonias loved water. But with the evening's watering they took strength again and a little freshness, and all of them prevailed against the sun. Mrs Chandles tried hard to keep them fresh and they troubled her a great deal, and I knew that because of this, too, she prayed for the rains.

Mrs Chandles kept saying no July heat was ever like this, and this was the worst July ever, but she always said such things and I did not believe. I knew the rains would start any time now but I did not know when, and I could not help looking up at the laden sky and wondering when. Not that I was anxious for rain.

Then in class one day we all jumped because of a sudden noise and it was thunder, and the thunder cracked again and we all put our hands to our ears. Two or three stunning peals followed and then there was a flash of lightning and the lightning seemed to stay still for a moment and it made a big fork in the sky. A girl shrieked. The teacher did not say anything but went to close the window. As he closed it the thunder came rumbling from far and then cracked as if it wished to split the earth. In spite of all that Mr Langley did not pull the window shut but held it half-open and peeped out at the sky. 'Whew!' he said, and we laughed. The girl who had shrieked was very jittery and excited and she laughed at everything and it looked as though she was waiting for more thunder, to shriek again. Behind me there was a thick-paned glass window. It framed the small view of the sky and I saw now this picture of the sky was not blue and light but the colour of slate. Thunder cracked again and again we jumped. There was a shutter over this thick-paned window. Mr Langley came now to pull it down. He asked us if we wanted it down. Half the class said yes, and half said no. Mr Langley pulled it down. Those who had said yes, laughed uproariously, and Mr Langley laughed too. The jittery girl talked loudly as if she didn't care. Mr Langley did not say anything to her. The class went on like this and everybody felt excited and cosy. And then we began to hear an occasional tap-tap, and then a low drumming, and then the rains broke violently upon the roof. There was not so much noise in class now. I, for one, was thinking of the rainy season.

After evening prayers and the school was dismissed there was no great rush for the gates. I stood near to Learie in the crowd and we sheltered under the overhanging eaves, but several children went home through the rain. Barrington, who sat at the back desk as a rule, stood with us. Barrington lived just on the other side of the main road. We could see his house from where we were standing. It was a nice house but Barrington never appeared to us to be living there. But he was living there.

'Barrington!' Learie shouted. 'Barrington you getting wet in de rain!' This Barrington was the biggest boy in our class and he sat at the back desk and Mr Langley was very proud of him and always patting him round the head because he said he never met a boy who was dunce as that. Barrington was always laughing. He laughed now and eased a little from where the rain was blowing in. Everybody was looking at him. Learie had said that for the purpose. Big Barrington drew nearer to us and Learie said, 'Look at Barry. 'E living jes across dey and 'e sheltering from rain!'

There was loud laughter at this and everybody kept looking at Barrington to see how silly he was because he was sheltering from rain, but Barrington grinned back and seemed very pleased.

Learie always did this sort of thing. He made fools of everybody, especially Barrington. He did that even to me. And I was his friend. It always occurred to me, how was it he made people laugh like that? People laughed at everything he said. The class was always on his side. I looked at him now and I knew he was thinking of some mischief. He looked at me. I laughed. Then he made believe he was looking at the rain. When he glanced and saw that Barrington wasn't watching he slipped quietly to the back of him. Then he pushed him suddenly into the rain. 'Barrington yuh modder calling yuh!' he cried. The children roared. Some screamed.

The rains had been pouring down hard and water was running over from the over-filled spouts of the school-house. It was splashing down continuously on to the concrete yard. Learie had pushed Barrington into this and there was Barrington taking a good wetting and a riot of cheers went up at this and when Barrington tried to jump back into a sheltering place the other boys stood up there waiting to push him back again. He stood for a moment in the pouring rain, confused and grinning, and getting soaking wet. There was pandemonium among the pupils and some of the girls watching screamed with delight. Barrington stood there just for a short moment and then he turned and dashed through the downpour for home. The laughter was deafening. That was a great session for the school.

That evening I, too, got wet. Learie and I had run over to Barrington's place and we each got an old jacket of Barrington's father and we went home through the rain with those. We turned left, along Rushworth Street, and running down the hill the winds pelted the rains into our faces. I drank some of it. I was holding the jacket mostly over my head. The front of my shirt was so wet, it clung to my body. We passed all the shops and the little café that sold the big ice-cream blocks for one cent, but nobody seemed to be in these places. We turned towards Browne Lane and Learie was home. So I ran on alone in the blinding rain and I noticed how big the drops were falling and I watched how much vapour was steaming up from the pitch because the pitch had been so hot. Coming into Cascade Street, I did not even dream of standing up in front of Julia's house, but dashed across into Romaine Street. I was panting so much I had to walk a little. I was weak and dripping. The jacket had not been of much use. When you ran against the rains you seemed to get soaked twice as quickly. I did not care how much wetter I got now. I was still blowing and my arms were so tired I held the jacket down to rest my arms and I let the rains do whatever they wanted. Here was our gate now and I weakly pushed it open. My shoes were going blotch! blotch! because of the water in them and water was streaming from my hair down the back of my neck and over my face. I left my shoes on the back step and went with my dripping clothes into the house.

TWENTY-TWO

Rain fell all that evening. After changing my clothes in the passage – standing on newspapers Mrs Chandles had hastily brought out – I went into the kitchen with dry clothes and was feeling good. Mrs Chandles was kneading dough. She asked me had I dried my head properly. I said yes. I could see she was in a good mood. The kitchen was clean and nice and the window was closed and there was the sense of being shut in cosily. I looked at Mrs Chandles kneading the dough and I wondered how often she had ever kneaded dough since I came here. Maybe only once or twice. Somehow she made me think of my mother kneading dough. I wondered what exactly was she going to make, whether it was roast or fried bakes. When she began to lay it out I would know. The oil stove was alight and Mrs Chandles gave me the kitchen-cloth and she said, Wipe out the big pot. She put another pot on the fire and there was water in it and I knew tonight we would be having chocolate tea. When it was going to be green tea she put on the kettle to boil and drew the tea in the teapot. It was going to be chocolate tea tonight. I was glad. Chocolate tea and bakes used to be my favourite at Mayaro. I knew what sort of bakes it was going to be now. She was cutting off pieces of dough and flattening them out round. It was going to be fry-bakes and chocolate tea tonight. It was very cool so I rubbed my hands together. The rains were still running riot on the galvanized roof. It was nice and cheerful in the kitchen. I was feeling glad.

I went to the window and I opened it a little and Mrs Chandles didn't say anything. The sky was slate-grey with rain and the rain fell densely over the town. The far houses were obscured with mist. Down in Celesta Street I could see the water rushing along the sides of the pavement and streaming into the middle of the street. The wind held the rains slantingly and it puffed some fine water into my face. I drew my head in. I looked towards the cane-lands to see how it was over there, but it was no use – the mist was thick in the distance. The town was very still except for the noise of water falling. It was as if everything had moved out to some other part and as if life had stopped for a while. I closed the window again.

Mrs Chandles looked at me as if to say she had known this would come, all along. I had the feeling that she did not want to talk. Sometimes when people were glad they did not want to talk. The water was on the boil and Mrs Chandles opened the cupboard and was searching in it. She brought out a grater and a ball of chocolate and she held the grater and chocolate over the pot and grated vigorously with the fine chocolate falling in. The grater was very tiny. I looked at it and I smiled. It had been used only a very few times and it always made me smile. Mrs Chandles went to the tray and lifted the cloth off the flat, white dough-bakes and at that moment it was a good thing my eyes had travelled back to the pot on the fire. I rushed and turned the stove off and the chocolate rose right up to the edge and stayed there for a moment then went down again. 'Oo!' Mrs Chandles cried, 'Good thing you so quick, boy!' The chocolate was smelling very pleasant. She took the pot down and I struck a match and lit the stove again. I was feeling glad of what I had done. And I was glad how Mrs Chandles had spoken to me. We were good friends. You knew when you were good friends with people although you weren't saying much. Mrs Chandles put some oil in the big pot and put it on the fire. While it was getting hot she pricked a pattern of fork-marks on the pieces of flat round dough.

I knew she was very happy because of the rains. She had said, 'God! look at this weather!' but I knew she was pleased about it. She was not even angry about my coming into the house with dripping clothes. She had said, 'That was thunder, eh! Jeesus!' Already she had seemed fresher for the coolness of the evening. There was not the bewildered and irritated look which the hotness of the day gave her. The tumult outside brightened her up. Any time now I expected her to say this was the worst rains she had seen. I waited, almost amused to hear that. She moved about the kitchen with zeal. I looked at her.

I went into the dining-room and there were two or three bits of paper on the floor and I took them up. I came out into the kitchen and put them into the bin. There were a few things about that could be washed up. I put them into the sink and did that. I went and tidied up the passage and there was not much for me to do now but I did what little there was. Then I came back into the kitchen, where Mrs Chandles was, and opening the window a little again I watched the rains still beating down furiously, and I watched how the water was collecting in hollow parts of the school grounds.

There was nobody about. Every now and again I would hear a noise at the front of our house and it would be a car going by on Romaine Street. The noise of the engine would barely be above that of the rains but you could hear clearly the swish-swish of water that spun off the wheels.

And then after a little while, something amused me in Celesta Street. The man who lived in one of the near houses came speeding home on a bicycle. He was covered from head to saddle with a big old jacket. In front of him there was a rice-bag tied like a baby's napkin and the tail of it was hanging over the handle-bar. He looked soaking wet. He must have pulled too hard on the brakes for the bicycle tyres screeched and before they came to a stop the bicycle skidded and they were both on the ground. The man got up from the ground quickly and lifted the bicycle high and ran under the house with it. He leaned it up against a post. Then he rushed back to the front, taking a little more wetting as he did so, and he ran up the front steps of his house. Then he stood up in the veranda untying the rice-bag from his neck and taking off the dripping jacket. Then he looked back at the place where he had fallen, and he looked to see if anybody was watching, then he looked out at the weather and went inside. I laughed. I saw no one else in the rain. The man was the only cheerful sight on Celesta Street.

I closed the window once more. Mrs Chandles did not hear me laugh. I did not tell her about the man. It was odd how at times you could keep a joke to yourself and at other times you could not, you had to tell somebody. It was odd, too, how Mrs Chandles was in a good mood and she did not want to say anything. When she was in a bad mood these days she did not say anything either. I wondered if it was a new custom she was taking up or if it was just that she was feeling not to talk. That's funny, I thought. But I could tell she was very easy with me.

The bakes were frying now and they too were making a racket in the place. Every time a new bit of dough hit the pot the oil went 'Shee-a, shee-a', and when, being already browned on one side, it was turned on the other, it made the same noise again. It was very nice being in the kitchen and smelling the frying bakes and the chocolate tea. I leaned up with my back to the closed window and I looked at all that was going on. I felt my head to see if my hair was very dry but when your hands had just been in water you could not tell whether your hair was very dry. But I knew I had rubbed and rubbed it with the towel and my hair should be dry enough.

The bakes were nearly all fried now. In fact only the last batch was in the pot. Mrs Chandles turned the fire low. She rubbed her hands together and she went and opened the window a bit.

I said: 'This rain wouldn't pass at all!'

'No,' she said. 'Nice weather for ducks.'

'If it keep on so till tomorrow—'

I was thinking that if it kept on so till tomorrow morning I could not go to school. But of course I would go to school. Because if it rained like this tomorrow morning there would be only half the class present and there wouldn't be any classwork to do, and we would laugh and talk all the time, and if Barrington came, Learic would be in his glory and he'd make us choke for laughing. I would want to go to school so I changed the subject.

'This is a sudden rainy season,' I said.

'Remember it's July!' Mrs Chandles was quick on this point. She turned to me and her finger pointed out it was July. 'Remember how long now crop finish. Don't forget that!'

'True,' I said.

Mrs Chandles turned the fire off because the bakes were finished. Something else came to my mind.

'Last year at Mayaro rain caused lots of floods.'

She didn't dispute it. She looked at me as if to say these things do happen. Then she spoke of many disasters in times when it rained and rained and rained.

She sat cosily and we talked. She said she didn't mind the rains at all, but when you had the sun blazing down day after day it could drive you crazy. I agreed with her, although, secretly, I could never have too much of the sun and the dry season. I told her about the dry season at Mayaro, and just to speak of it, I seemed to feel the stinging heat again, and to see the destruction of the bush behind our house. I remembered the poui, and I told her about the poui flowers in the hills, when the dry season was ending.

Both the yellow poui and the passion poui set the hills aflame with flowers. And then there were the immortelles. There was no taller tree in the forest than the immortelle tree, and no flower redder than the immortelle flower. From the window the hills seemed afire with both immortelle and poui, and from there too you heard the cry of the cigala, and the rains were near.

Mrs Chandles was looking at me, and then I realized I was getting excited and we both laughed. Off and on she had been attending to the supper and she got up now to see. As she hobbled to the stove I wanted to ask her when and how did she happen to fall and hurt herself. But I did not ask. She went into the dining-room and started laying the table. She began telling me of something that happened one dry season a long, long time ago. I listened and I looked away for this was too much to swallow. Her eyes looked quite playful and quaint. I smiled to myself and then I thought, maybe such things happened!

TWENTY-THREE

At supper we sat rather silently and we ate and listened to the water falling. The chocolate was very delicious. I had the last bake on my plate now, and fish from the midday cooking. I ate almost hungrily and I wondered if it was pouring down at Mayaro now. It was already July. Who would believe it?

I could hear the water pouring down the spout on the roof on to the concrete drain. My thoughts were far away. Who would be-lieve it? July! Only a little while back I had arrived in this place. The crop had not even come yet. Now it had come and gone. Now the rains were falling. Half a year had gone.

'What you studying about?'

The old lady's voice all but made me jump. 'Nothing – just Mayaro.'

'You always studying about Mayaro. And hand under chin. You is an old man or what?'

The rain outside seemed to isolate us from everything. It seemed to bind us together in a strange way and to make us more relaxed with each other. It even seemed to be making relatives of us. I hoped this would not change but would remain as it was. And yet I knew it would change. I knew there was a name for the way we were feeling and that this feeling came from the weather. I sensed this rather than knew it because when I had looked out at the town through the kitchen window and had seen nobody in the rain I had felt the rain had cut off everybody and I had known a certain nearness for the people in the town. I felt this nearness to Mrs Chandles now for the rain had cut us off from everything and had left us together.

I tried to guess what Mrs Chandles was feeling about the weather. Her legs would be all right now. I wondered how was it that the heat had affected her like that and made her legs bad.

I felt was she being so good to me because she was glad of this cool weather. These months I had handled the market job in a manner which pleased her. She had said something I would not easily forget. She had said I was as good as Brinetta, if not better. I didn't know if I had wanted to be better than Brinetta. Perhaps I had. This thought confused me. Perhaps I wanted to be the best of all.

We both sat there eating and Mrs Chandles did not say anything else. Perhaps she, too, was thinking of private things. My mind travelled to that far ramshackle house and I wondered if it was raining over there and if the water was coming through the roof. That roof was like a sift, and getting worse.

I was thinking about all this and afterwards I raised my head and discovered the old lady's eyes on me again. Lately she had said I was always thinking of Mayaro. She had said I'd never be a town-boy if I kept on like that. As she looked at me now I said, 'This rain isn't stopping!'

'That's good,' she said. 'Keep everything cool and quiet. You see how the school-yard is? Not a sound.'

I listened to the drumming on the roof-top. On a chair in the drawing-room I could see a copy of the *Illustrated London News*. Each week Mr Chandles brought them from La Brea to read about the war. I thought of getting up and going to wash up the few things, but it was so cosy I remained seated. I sat in silence and let all sorts of things go through my mind. After a while I became aware of the deadened sound above and I raised my head.

'Ah, it's going,' I said.

I got up and opened the window just a little. The rain was only drizzling now and in the yard there was much water and the drain was overfull and the water was flowing out underneath the house, I watched the water running down in the drain and the bits of wood and paper that sailed busily with it and in places where water was overflowing bits of wood and paper were stranded, like ships, on the concrete edge.

I leaned over and looked to see how wet underneath the house was. As I bent, looking, powdery rain was sprinkling the back of my neck. It was hardly wetting me. The drizzle had almost completely faded out. I straightened from the bending and looked up at the sky. I turned quickly to Mrs Chandles. Where the skies had cleared you never saw a rainbow so bright.

'Rainbow!' I said.

Mrs Chandles thoughts must have been far away. She said, 'Eh?'

'Look, a rainbow!'

She came to the window. Standing beside me she stuck her head out then drew it in again quickly, then she put her hand out to test how heavy the drizzle was. Then seeing it was hardly drizzling at all she stuck out her head like a peacock and looked up.

I pointed, 'Across there. In front of you.' It was as big as the world in front of the window but she was searching for it.

'Oh!' she said.

That was all she said.

We stood up for some time looking at it. The sky there was light and showed up the colours boldly. We could see only the top part of the arch. At Mayaro if you were on the beach you could see the whole arch. Every time it rained there were rainbows over the sea. They had looked as bright as this one and they had stood there, both feet in the water. This one had appeared so suddenly. It had appeared while we were sitting there eating. It was the first rainbow of the season. The rains had hardly passed but here was a rainbow to tell of more rains. Mrs Chandles watched it keenly, as though this brought back something to mind, then she said:

'My heart leaps up when I behold—' and she paused.

'What's that?'

'Wordsworth.'

'Wordsworth?'

'You don't learn poetry at school or what?'

I did not quite understand and I said nothing. We did learn poetry at school. She remained there looking at the skies and the only sound was the sound of the drizzling rain. At length she said, 'Well plenty more water on the way.'

Yes, there was plenty more rain on the way. But I knew that after the first strangeness there would be no more joy in the rains. In the streets there would be puddles so you could easily put your foot into them and when the cars went by you had to jump away from the spurt of muddy water. And at school there would be no cricket at lunchtime because the ground would be wet and soggy like a mud-hog's basin. That was what the rains would mean from tomorrow, although it would be fine to be at home in the night and to lie down with darkness on top and below and to listen to the water making havoc on the roof and on the whole world outside.

'Chilly!' Mrs Chandles said. She had both arms folded in front of her and she cringed up her shoulders. She was very thin. Her thinness stood out quite a lot these days I wondered how old could she be. She had talked often of her thinness. She had said she was falling away like anything. She had said she wasn't well at all. I had never paid much attention to that but I saw now she was really falling away. Her dress hung on her like a sugar-bag. When I first came here you could not have said she was fat but she was not anything like she was now.

'You'll fix up everything, eh,' she said, 'and lock up the back door. I'm going in early tonight. You all right?'

'Yes.'

'The gallery chilly like *France*. You'll lock up, eh?'

'Yes, Mrs Chandles.'

It was good when she talked that way. When she talked to me like that it made me feel I could lock up right away or do any work and when I was in that mood I could do things good. When she used to shout at me it had made me very nervous. I did silly things then. Not on purpose. It just made me stupid when she bawled at me.

I put the light on in the dining-room. Outside now it was dark. The evenings always went quickly but now that it rained there seemed to have been no evening at all. I pulled in the dining-room window and latched it. Then I took up the cups and saucers and plates and went to the sink with them and after I had shaken the table-cloth crumbs out of the kitchen window I washed up the plates and cups and saucers right away. Then I stood up a little looking out on Celesta Street. Across the lights I noticed a shimmering and I knew the rains were drizzling again.

It was indeed chilly – but not in an uncomfortable way. Mrs Chandles could not stand the chill because she was old and maybe she was falling away. She could not stand the heat either. It was funny but it was that way with ageing people. I wondered if Mrs Chandles was near a hundred. When the weather was cool it was better for her legs. Yet Ma had a sore leg once and it was the rainy weather she could not stand. It made the sore itch. But the hot weather was all right. It could never be too hot for Ma. Mrs Chandles preferred the rains but after a little while it had made her solemn and not wanting to talk, and she had noticed the chill. Ma liked the sun and perhaps everybody else did, except Mrs Chandles. Ma used to wash clothes over a tub in the hot sun and sing. I remember the washing distinctly, and the singing.

I wished I could just forget about such things for now. If I just thought about the town and about the school things would be all right. Tomorrow there would be nothing doing in the playground. It would be too muddy. We could stay in the garden shed, then, and watch the tractors move earth away for that new road. The tractors liked mud. And they grunted too, and then they bored their noses in. Next year there might be cars speeding where there were tractors working now. There would be cars passing right behind the school. The road was going to join up Cross Crossing with the Rushworth Street side of the town. It would be very exciting to have a busy new road passing just behind the school. We were glad of this. Although the tractors were to level off part of our playing-fields, because the road would be passing there. That was not *our* playing-fields, really, but we went all down there to play. Mr Soames always said our school-grounds were big enough, but we went much further out, and during the crop we used to go down to the train line to wait for the estate cane-wagons, to rob them of cane. When Mr Soames found that out and got the boys' names he gave very good benchings for that. If the boy was small, instead of putting him across a bench he would put him across his own lap, and lowering the boy's pants he would whip him till there were weals all over the boy's behind. No boy would be too small to be benched if he was not too small to raid the cane-wagons. We were terrified of the benchings.

Thinking of benchings, I passed my hands across the seat of my pants. It was a long time since I last got one. There were no more cane-wagons now, and with the tractors working there would be no more going down to the lines anyway. Good luck to Mr Soames!

There was just nothing more to do now, I had finished all there was. Yet it seemed as if I hadn't done anything all evening. It was the break from watering the plants that caused that. I went for my wet shirt and pants and went downstairs to the bathroom and hung them up to dry. I got sprinkled as I walked down the back steps. It was not late now but with the rains the night had been dark a long time. I wished I was allowed to play the radio. I felt like listening to music or something. Anyway, I'd better go for my bedding, I thought. I'd better go for my bedding and spread them out thick and lie down. In the quietness all sorts of thoughts kept floating into my head. One car, two cars, passed along Romaine Street. I could hear the water spinning off their wheels. Perhaps the drivers were thinking, What a night, what a time! I had the feeling to go in the veranda and look out. I went for a while but there was nothing to see except the darkness and the street lights yellowing small circles, and the louder humming of the rains. I didn't even switch on the veranda light to look at the plants. I went in and made my bed and lay down.

TWENTY-FOUR

The rains fell and stopped and fell and stopped all that week. And they went on like this through the next week and the next. It rained this way all the time. It was no surprise to see a rainbow now. They seemed to live in the sky.

And yet there were moments when the sun came out hotly again. It fell on things in a strange way, and the brightness looked yellow on the wet streets and on the wet houses, and though there was some heat in the sun you did not get the feeling that things were ever going to get dry again.

I had never seen rain fall so fiercely, nor had I seen so much. I had stood in the veranda at times and watched the Mount Naparaima, dark and forbidding, rain-mist obscuring the trees, and when I had heard the showers coming, bringing an ominous sound from the mountain itself, I had been made timid and I had feared there might be some disaster from the rains. But no such thing ever happened. And it must have been true, what people said, that San Fernando was shaped like a duck's back and the water only slid off it.

Now, one day, in the Geography class at school, Mr Langley was discussing rainfall, and I promptly put up my hand. All eyes turned to me, and Mr Langley was giving me attention, and I said, 'Sir, the mountain, Sir, *that* causes heavy rains.'

Mr Langley waited for the rumbles in the class to die down. Sometimes, if Mr Langley was in a certain mood and a boy said something silly, he would make a reply to set the class rolling with laughter. But if it was something sensible the boy had said he would praise the boy and be especially cheerful with him and the rest of the class would be made to look like idiots. But there were times when he was just mild. He was mild now, but you could see that he was looking at me closely.

'That's right,' he said.

The astonished faces looked round at me. I was embarrassed and glad. And Mr Langley, noticing, said, 'But only to a certain extent.' He took a piece of chalk and went to the blackboard and he drew the mountains, the winds and the rains and he showed what resulted when certain things happened. He went on a while about it, and after he had spoken of 'contours', and 'conditions', and 'isobars', and 'other factors', it turned out that the mountain had precious little to do with the rains. He explained the rains in a very unexpected way. He said it was the season for them.

The coolness of the days seemed like balm to Mrs Chandles' temper and she was hardly ever harsh with me. Mr Chandles arrived on week-ends and as usual he found fault with everything, but even Mrs Chandles seemed to slip out of his way and there were no more big quarrels in the house.

I did less work, too. I went to the market only now and again. Sometimes, with the cosiness and showers of the early morning with the rain making me lazier and more sleepful, I had to wring myself from bed to go to the market. I would knock on Mrs Chandles door to say I was ready and she would ask how hard was it raining. *Hard*, I would say. And usually she would say, 'Okay, don't bother if it falling so hard.'

There was no watering of plants either. Not even of the veranda ones, nor the ones in the wire-baskets. In fact everything in wire-baskets and flower-pots and out in the yard, were seeing their great days. The morning glory flaunted bright red flowers, and the begonias spread out thick and undignified, sending up tall flower-stalks to overshadow smaller plants. But the prim anthuriums were the pride of the veranda. These gave Mrs Chandles much pleasure, and so did the roses. If I were walking down the front steps there would be roses on either side of me.

It seemed very odd that at this time, when people went about so busily, with umbrellas, and kept watching the skies, hastening to avoid showers soon to fall – it seemed to me odd that now flowers should be overflowing in the town. For hardly anybody could stand up to look. The flowers gave brightness to the houses and to the streets, and often, standing at the kitchen window, I recognized the smells of some that I could name. These scents came on the wind mostly from Celesta Street. Looking at the verandas of those houses I always felt a tinge of envy for I had never seen the people there watering any plants and here were some of the finest flowers that ever saw light. But even these went unnoticed. Hardly anyone lingered in the streets.

The weeks of wet weather continued, with an occasional bright day, and one such Saturday morning, on receiving a letter, Mrs Chandles called to me.

'Have a little job for you,' she said.

'Yes.'

'It's to go down to see Edwin for me. All right?'

'Yes, Mrs Chandles.'

I was thrilled. Edwin had come a few times since Easter. He had worn a hat, because of the weather, and he had looked funny in it. He was always big and strapping and in a hurry. It was very pleasant when he came.

Mrs Chandles went and fetched a writing pad and went and sat at the table. I watched her writing. I didn't know what exactly was going on but there was a lot going on, for on the occasions when Edwin had come I had overheard talk about 'solicitors', and about 'deed', and 'the house'. In a way it had seemed there was a calm in the dispute with Mr Chandles, but really there was no calm, Edwin and the old lady were working without rest. I knew. I was secretly pleased and I wished them joy.

After a while Mrs Chandles looked up and saw me and she said, as if to herself. 'This boy is always deep in thought.' I moved off, and she said, 'Well you'd better get ready, eh, Francis, in the meantime.'

'Yes, Mrs Chandles.'

I was quickly dressed and she gave me the letter and I hurried out. I walked along the Coffee Street and the sun was brightly yellow on the pitch and on the house-tops. There were many shoppers about and I eased through them and went on until I came to the High Street. Here, I had never been before and here was all the grandeur of the town. The big stores rose up beside me and I walked beneath their overhangs and I felt very daring to be here all on my own. In the street there was a mêlée of traffic and there were thousands of people on the pavements and in the shops. I thought I was good for myself, but this was a completely strange world to me. I walked down until I came to a big swing in the High Street and now just before me were the great engineering houses of which everyone knew. On either side the road widened and I could see that just behind the engineering houses was the wharf. I walked across to the engineering shop and asked for Edwin Chandles.

After a short while Edwin appeared at the counter and when he saw it was me he glanced over his shoulders, both sides, and he looked very secretive. I gave him the letter and he tore it open and read it right there. He kept saying, 'Good, good!' as he came to certain parts of it, and at the end he said 'Good, that's the feller!' and he said to me, 'Give me a chance, Franco, let me get a pencil and I'll fix up a note.' He went in and came back out quickly. He looked even broader and more strapping in his overalls. I wondered what would happen if he and Mr Chandles came to grips. It was a terrifying thought.

'There you are!' he said. 'Just a little scribble, and something inside for the old-girl.' He folded the piece of paper and gave it to me. There was money in it. He didn't need an envelope to put it in. He trusted me. I put it carefully in my pocket.

'So how's tricks,' he said, 'Everything okay?'

'Yes,' I said.

'Noah home yet?'

I was puzzled.

He burst out laughing. 'You don't know who Noah is?' and he laughed heartily again.

'No,' I said. I couldn't help laughing for watching him laugh.

'Well you is a hell of a man if you don't know Noah. That's your boss – Noah – the man who knows everything. The man-about-town.' He was still laughing and I lost all my embarrassment and was laughing too.

I said, 'He ain't home yet.'

'He might be there when you get back. Now, Franco, be careful how you hand Mother that note, for God's sake.'

'Okay.'

'Okay? Matter fix?'

'Yes.'

He put out his hand to me and I thought he was going to shake it, but I felt something hard, and when I opened my palm there was a shilling in it.

'Cheerio,' he said.

'Cheerio.'

'Watch it with the traffic.'

Instead of turning for home I walked round the engineering buildings towards the wharves. I had come too near to the gulf to go home again without seeing it. As I walked round the building I looked into the show-windows for I had heard so much about this place. They were supposed to fit ships and make nuts and bolts and files and shovels, and electrical parts and tractors and I did not know what in engineering they were not supposed to make. As I got past the building the road seemed to open into a big square, and down there in front of me was the wharf.

I walked amidst the thicker crowds of people, near the many cafés and the All Nations Seamen's Hostel, and I saw the row of custom houses and the long iron railings that fenced off some railway lines. And walking further in the direction of the railings I saw the bus terminals before me, bright with the buses that went to all parts of the country. There were the rows of yellow Princes Town buses facing one way, and the rows of blue Siparia buses facing another, and so many other buses in the middle of the busy waterfront place. I passed the buses and there before me and over the railings was the gulf. I watched it with my heart thumping and I hardly noticed that the big place to the right was the railway station. Locomotives were puffing and hissing and being shunted on to different lines and they seemed to be pulling wagons all over the place. I reached the iron railings and I stood there, watching the sea.

The sea lay like a blue blanket. To the right, I could not see much of it as the railway buildings blocked the view, but I watched it sprawling away to the horizon, and to the left I could see at some point down how the coast jutted out and my eyes followed the coast as far as was possible to see. I looked again in front of me and at the horizon and I noticed how the sky just above the water seemed splashed with blood. And I remembered that Easter evening again. Although it shone, the sun was not plainly seen, for the gathering clouds half-obscured it. It was now midway between tall sky and sea, and where the sky was clear around it the place was very red, and some of the clouds looked black-red, but the light that fell on the water was as red as blood. I turned away a little from the light and I looked at the towering buildings around and about me. The sunset light was falling upon the wharf too. To the left, and by the sea part of the railings, was the Fish Market. People had always talked about going down to the wharf for fish. On mornings, when the fish had been too expensive at the big market they had said it was murder, and they'd go down to the wharf. So here was where the Fish Market was. Now I knew. Now I knew, also, where the well-known lumber people were. So when the big lumber lorries passed down Romaine Street, I would know about them and where they came from.

Before the front part of the railway station and on the other side of the railway lines, was the jetty. It ran only a little way out in the water and at the end of it was a building which I supposed was the famous Boat House. If this was the Boat House I was very surprised for I had not expected anything as tumbling-down as this. The Boat House had a reputation for holiday fairs and dances and also for swimming clubs, and people said that the swimming clubs' regatta held on New Year's Day was the biggest show in the town.

After standing there for a little while I suddenly had the feeling to go over to the jetty, and then I thought, no, I'd better be going back home now. I thought I should have gone over there in the first place instead of waiting till now. There was a man standing on what looked like the very edge of the wharf and I wished I could go over there and do like him. But I could not go now. It had suddenly come to me how long I had left home. I wondered if Mrs Chandles would make a fuss.

I stood, still watching, unwilling to tear myself away and hurry home. The sun was clearly lower and the light was more sweeping over the sea. It tinted all the waterfront. I looked at where the sea and sky met and I wondered why couldn't I see Venezuela if Venezuela was just where the sea and sky met, across there. I had heard that on very clear days you could even see trees over there. The sun was showing a little and the edge was so bright you couldn't watch it for more than a moment. From the sea behind the Fish Market things like masts were showing above the roofs. I guessed they were of the lighters that came from Venezuela and from the Caribbean Sea. I still stood there watching.

I looked around to see if there was any clock showing. I could not spot any. Mount Naparaima towered above the red roofs. It looked aloof and gloomy and the trees were dark with the dusk. I could see mist hanging over the top. Mist, as distinct from dusk, grey like rain. Over the sea the sun was almost touching the water now. There was the feeling of things in the wind – the feeling that rain was close. Hundreds of people were milling about the wharf. It was time for me to go home. I would have to fly.

Just before I turned away I noticed that the gates which opened on to the railway tracks and to the jetty side of the wharf, were being shut. Another gate further down and in front the Fish Market was being shut too. And presently I became aware of a noise drawing nearer and nearer and I knew what was happening.

The train, far away to the left, came taking the bend gracefully, making itself into a semi-circle, then straightening out again. Every moment it grew bigger and bigger and then it passed the signal box and passed the Fish Market, and it came pelting in with a great clatter. It gave a long shriek and then it seemed to be slowing down. Carriages seemed to be forever passing, banging into one another and losing speed. And then the train stopped. I peeped beside the railing trying to see the people getting off and those getting on. And then I thought, Christ! I'd better go home *now*.

The place was more confusing because there seemed to be so many more people on the wharf now. And the buses appeared to have changed their positions altogether. I walked quickly and I felt confused as to which direction I had come from. And then I stopped and asked a man which way was the High Street. 'What!' he said. He was severe and impatient and did not wait for me to ask it again. He said to someone, 'Look at this young generation, children begging for money on the wharf!' The other man turned round to look at me. He raised his hands as if to drive me off. He said something which I did not hear. I kept my eyes on the line of shops, hoping to spot the engineering works. There were so many lines of shops about here. If I saw the engineering shop I would know exactly how to go. Many of the business places were already closed and those that were still open were brightly lit. The buses with their big headlights turned down from the wide corner, and passing where I was they headed for the railway station. As I looked back at them I noticed there were lights on the water too. It might have been the Boat House lights. Presently I came right against the engineering works, and then there before me was the High Street.

I hastened along it. The darkness was thin and the Mount Naparaima stood against it, darker and seeming very near. The evening was hot and I felt I was beginning to perspire. There was no wind at all. I heard a rumble but I could not be sure whether it was thunder because there were so many noises about. People called to each other loudly and there was the laughter of women in the upstairs veranda of a hotel. There were also women looking down into the street from a Chinese restaurant. There was much chatter and laughter among them. The sailors stood up in the street looking up at the restaurant. The women were saying things to them. The sailors were very drunk. I hurried along up the High Street and then I saw a clock hanging right over the pavement. I could not yet see the time. I glanced back down the High Street and I saw the two drunken sailors going into the restaurant.

TWENTY-FIVE

On coming into the house I was very timid to approach Mrs Chandles. It was several hours I had been away. Of course I had known exactly what excuse I was going to make but I was not sure how Mrs Chandles would take it. I went into the house and I came upon her in the dining-room. I stood up and stammered and couldn't bring out the words.

'What happen to you, Francis?' she said. 'Where you come from now!'

I told her that when I had got down to Edwin he was out and I waited till he came.

'Good God!' she said, 'I thought you got knock down or something!'

She looked very strained. She asked, 'He said anything?'

94

'Oh,' I said. I had nearly forgotten. I took out the folded paper and gave it to her.

'All right,' she said, 'thanks.'

I went to the kitchen feeling so relieved. I drank a big tumbler of water, then filled the glass to half again and drank. My face felt greasy with perspiration. I was not so tired, though. Remembering it was Saturday I wondered if Mr Chandles was in the house. I had forgotten him altogether. I became a little scared now and hoped he hadn't been in all the afternoon. The way Mrs Chandles had talked freely made me feel he wasn't in now and that he didn't know I had been away long. I stood up at the sink a little. Mrs Chandles came into the kitchen. She still looked strained and anxious. She said, 'If you didn't stay away so long – hm – you missed something.'

I waited for her to go on. But the next thing she said was more to herself than to me. It was said under her breath: 'Blasted scum!' I pretended I didn't hear. I went out to the back steps. I wondered what had happened while I was away.

Something was always happening here. I wondered what was it this time. The first person my mind went to was Julia. But it was so unlikely that these two would clash. Yet who else could it be? But what could Julia have done? Apart from those two occasions I had never seen Julia on the premises. I could not see how these two could have any disturbance with each other. I did not think she could be referring to Julia at all. But it was possible.

I tried to think of other things that were possible. Was it some letter that came, then? Could it be an angry letter from Brinetta, for instance? This surely was impossible. In any case she wouldn't call Brinetta that. It couldn't be any such thing.

I thought to myself, why worry, I had stayed away so late and everything was all right. I was so relieved to get off as easily as that. What could have happened while I was away? It could be a letter that came from Marva to Mr Chandles and the old lady found it. Still, no private letters for Mr Chandles came here. All that came here were electric light bills and water-rate bills and you could easily tell those letters because they were in Council envelopes and had transparent sections in front. Then, too, when Mrs Chandles had been in good moods I had heard her talk of Mr Chandles' private letters and she had said that he was carrying on so much business that his private letters couldn't come here. I didn't think what happened had to do with any letter at all. I wondered what could it be. I wondered if it was not just the old age telling on Mrs Chandles.

But I thought that without really believing it. Mrs Chandles was perhaps more collective of mind than I was. The atmosphere still felt hot and heavy, and still there was no wind. It was very dark. I thought to myself that I had better look for something to do, as I had only just come in and Mrs Chandles was okay about it, but there was nothing to do, and I felt there was some uneasiness in the house. I walked back through the landing towards the back step. I suddenly heard footsteps coming through the dining-room. Then Mr Chandles appeared and went into the kitchen.

From the back steps I heard the drag of Mrs Chandles' slipper. I knew how it sounded on the ordinary wooden floor of the house and I knew how it sounded on the concrete of the kitchen. Immediately she was in the kitchen there came the sharpness of angry voices. The voices were harsh and crude and there was no effort to hide what was being said. It was exactly like what had happened that Easter morning.

I was very shocked but I listened. They were talking very loudly. At least Mrs Chandles knew I was in the house. Anyway I had seen her temper before and I knew that when she flared up she did not care who was about. I felt hot inside because of the things they were saying and I was sure that their voices were reaching to people in the nearby houses. Mr Chandles used expressions I never thought he had known. Above his voice the old lady's seemed to be screaming frenziedly at him. Her words were equally strong and very embarrassing. I was shocked more for the people in the surrounding houses than for anything else. Mrs Chandles' voice was toning down now. She seemed exhausted from her own anger but still she wasn't giving up.

'Not in this house!' she was saying now. 'Damn you, not in this house!' She said that about four or five times.

'Not in which house?' Mr Chandles bellowed after a while. 'You know who paying the rates? You know who paying the bills here? Check up on that!'

Mrs Chandles' silence seemed to fall heavily. But I felt she could have had a good reply to this. Even I knew that although Mr Chandles had been paying the rates, the deed for the house was in Mrs Chandles' name and he could not get her to alter it. But nevertheless he always claimed that the house was his, and that the Government knew who was paying the rates.

The row had been disturbing but this silence was very tense. I wondered if they would continue from here or if this was the end of it. And then I heard Mrs Chandles say, half to herself and in a reflective voice: 'Who would believe that! Who would believe he'd bring that trash in my house!'

Mr Chandles' reply was sharp and quick. 'Look who's talking!' he said. 'Look who's talking! You was so gentle and meek and mild, and what happen to Father, eh? What happen about that!' And he paused, a triumphant ring in his last words, and Mrs Chandles started up again and he cut in to challenge her and their voices joined together like the gabbling of geese, and I couldn't make out a single thing they were saying, and maybe it was just as well.

Still, I was thinking who did Mr Chandles bring to the house! I was certain it was Julia. Julia again! I thought. I wondered what had happened. In a way I was glad I had been out.

I walked down the steps and into the yard. Really, it was a long time since I had heard a quarrel like this. After Easter, I did not expect to hear another such quarrel in this house. I stood in the darkness of the yard and was thinking about it. I was a bit shaken but apart from that I could not tell exactly how I was feeling. In the darkness I walked along the side of the fence, past the w.c. Since I could not get a chance to weed these days, owing to the weather, the sweetbroom had sprung up surprisingly tall. Now they brushed against my legs in the dark. I reached the place where the side fence joined the back fence and I stood there aimlessly and looked down into Celesta Street. There was nothing to see but the darkness and the lit-up, many-coloured window panes. I stood up there, thinking.

After a while I tried to stop thinking of what had happened and I stooped and took up a few stones in my hand and was letting some fall through my fingers and I was thinking, Look what a little time it took for the sweetbroom to spring up so. If it was something useful or something that even bore a nice flower, you would have had to tend it carefully and do all sorts of things to it to get it to flourish like this. But because it was sweetbroom it just sprang up without any trouble.

I wondered if the neighbours had heard anything. It was not very late and there were lights in all the houses. These two people here! I thought. Good heavens!

I kept looking up at the window because hearing no sound it

occurred to me that Mr Chandles might have gone out again. I thought of going indoors. I let the rest of the little stones fall through my fingers and I flicked the bigger ones off in the dark. Never was there such a hot windless night. Never was there such a blank, cheerless sky. I was beginning to feel a little tired from the walking all afternoon and I wondered if Mr Chandles had gone out and I felt I would like to go in and have a sleep. But after a moment I saw Mr Chandles had not gone. His head appeared big and full under the kitchen lamp. I heard the tap running and the water being sucked down into the drain. Then his head was gone from under the light. So he was still in the house! Maybe he wasn't going anywhere tonight. Hell! I thought.

I wondered if I should be out here, with Mr Chandles being in the house. After all that had happened I thought I'd better keep near and do something useful. It was not so late but because of the weather it was pitch-black. I did not want to go into the house with Mr Chandles about. There was nothing to do there and it would take very little to start Mr Chandles shouting at me. I thought I knew what I could do. The day had been hot and I thought just to keep occupied I could sprinkle a few cans of water on the plants now. It wouldn't seem odd because we had often watered the plants at night, after the sun's heat had cooled. So this was a good idea because Mr Chandles would know I was in the house and he would see I was doing something. I went to the bathroom for the watering-can. I filled it and went round to the front.

From the veranda I could hear Mr Chandles walking about in his room. This brightened me because it looked as though he would be going out soon. I could tell by his walking in the room when he was going out. These days he used his room only as a base and no sooner he came into it, he hovered round a little and took off again.

I sprinkled the plants on the veranda very lightly because really, they did not need the water. The ones in the wire-basket, needed the water even less. Indeed those flourished so well that the old lady had threatened to use the shears on them. Even on the roses in the yard. Now in this darkness there were no flowers at all, only so many shadows. But the Ladies of the Night were unmistakable. They smelt very strongly. This made me think of yearning and enchantment and Julia and things I did not understand.

I stopped a little and laughed at my silly thinking, and then I jumped because the front door was pushed open. Then I heard Mr Chandles in the veranda. His footsteps were sounding double and when he came to the steps I straightened up and stood on the side, allowing him to pass. And then, turning round with the can, my heart gave a violent thump. Mr Chandles and Marva were going out through the gate.

TWENTY-SIX

That night the clouds broke. The rains came with such fury as was seldom seen in the town. I slept soundly because of the tiredness but twice I awoke and twice I heard the tumult of the rains outside. And the next morning the rains passed and left the water to run down the drains of the streets.

Marva I did not see again. When Mr Chandles had returned late that night I had not been asleep yet. He had come into the dining room and I was surprised because he spoke to me in a nice way.

'Sleeping?' he had said, switching on the light. At first I hadn't been sure it was *me* he was talking to.

'No,' I had said.

My head had been turned to the wall and I did not turn around to him because it was very embarrassing for me to have seen Marva come from the house. I was ashamed to look Mr Chandles in the face.

'Hot!' he had said, and he had whistled, 'Whew!' as the heat always made you do. 'It's this rain, you know.'

'Yes.'

There was a little pause and then he said, 'So how you liking San Fernando.'

'It's nice,' I said.

'And school? School all right? Old Soames still there?'

'Yes. Mr Soames still there. They say he'll be transferred.'

'Transferred? Well it's time, you know. After all.'

He stood there in the light, tall and big of bone, and I felt strange that I was so glad just because he was standing there talking with me. I realized if I had hated him enough I wouldn't have felt that way to talk to him now. I felt that perhaps this was what I had been hoping for all the time, not to be rid of him, but to have him being friendly to me. I had eased round and he stood looking down on me, never looking at my eyes directly, and I wondered if it was because I had seen him walk down the steps with Marva that he came to talk to me now. I lay there in the light under him, and I was feeling uneasy and I thought how very strange this was – here was Mr Chandles talking with me!

He walked round the table to the window. He unlatched it. I could see him looking up at the sky.

'Oh, this rain,' he said.

I wasn't hearing anything above.

I said, 'It falling?'

'No. But just you wait!' he said. He looked at me and smiled in a rather awkward way and his face had the expression which said he did not trust the rains.

I lay silent, beginning to feel easier, more comfortable.

'And it should be Indian Summer,' he said.

'Yes.'

In truth, September was the month of Indian Summer. Sometimes it came a little earlier, but usually this was the month for it. It was a nice time and the sun came out every day and you almost forgot you were in the rainy season.

'Anyway today was fairly bright.' He put out his head again and looked at the sky.

'*Very* bright,' I ventured, 'and hot.'

'It still hot,' he laughed. He pushed the window wide open, not seeming to realize I was lying in bed and that the draught was bad.

He said, 'Don't talk about rain, you'll get that from now till Christmas. Until Crop. You'll get steady rain from now till next Crop.'

The word 'Christmas' had rung in my mind and remained. I thought this was a good time to ask him. Lately I had been wondering if some miracle could happen and I could go home for Christmas.

'I wish I could go home for Christmas,' I said. I had never been so brave in all my life.

'Oh, you want to go home for Christmas. We'll see. Christmas will be a little busy here this year. Anyway, we'll see. Yes, I think you could go. We'll see.'

Joy had flowed like water through me and filled me up. I was so happy I did not know what to say. And then I said, 'Thanks, Mr Chandles.'

100

'It's all right,' he said. 'That's all right. I think I'd better leave you to get some sleep.'

For the rest of that week-end I did not see the same chumminess, but for a change he was not hostile towards me.

The hoped-for Indian Summer did not approach during the following week, although the sun came out more frequently, after the rains, and the days were dull, then bright, or rainy then bright, and often, rainy again. And sometimes at school, we knew the Devil and his Wife were fighting, for the rain and sun were both out at the same time. At school, too, when the thunder cracked loudly we jumped, and the excited girl squealed, and there would be uproar for a moment and Mr Langley would come to the back of the class and shut the window. Sometimes Miss Tomlin from the next class, would come over to find out what the noise was about. Miss Tomlin was a new teacher, transferred from a Port-of-Spain school, and she did not like much noise. She was young, but a high-grade teacher and I forgot what wonderful exams Mr Langley told us she had passed. As soon as she appeared Mr Langley would say, 'Less noise, Class! And Miss Tomlin would look at us through her glasses as if we had to keep quiet because she had come from a Port-of-Spain school. But she never said anything, and usually she would smile with Mr Langley and go back to her class again.

Once, in the back row, we were talking about Miss Tomlin. Some of the boys said she was nice-looking but Learie jeered at them and said he had a granny who was nice-looking too. There was a little argument about whether Miss Tomlin was nice-looking or not, then Learie asked Barrington where he would class-up Miss Tomlin. Barrington said, 'Who? She? With a crapaud!' The way he said this made the whole back desk roll with laughter. Mr Langley struck his whip on the table and said, 'Back row!' Mr Langley wasn't stern, really. He was trying to please Miss Tomlin. Anyway, Miss Tomlin wasn't bad-looking.

It must have been that very week when I felt crisp paper in my pocket. I couldn't guess what it was, and it had been there all the time and I had not thought about it. Anyway I emptied my pocket and I was glad I was alone when I did this. I was taken aback when I saw what was before me. It was the dollar-bill Edwin had folded into the note he had scribbled for Mrs Chandles. I had given Mrs Chandles the note, thinking it was still inside. This could be no other money.

I did not know what to do about this now. My first thought was to take it straight to Mrs Chandles. I could only say I had forgotten it, but I wasn't sure if she'd believe me. On my way home from school that afternoon I showed it to Learie and told him what had happened.

Learie's eyes bulged to see the money and he had great misgivings as to what Mrs Chandles would do with me if I handed it up.

'She might even call the police,' he said.

I was silent.

'They'll say you couldn't forget it all that time. This could be real trouble, boy.'

As he had said this, his face had shown all the horrors of what could befall me. But I was not all that silly. Learie just wanted us to go and have a spree with the dollar, that was all. But I held out against him.

Anyway I was not sure what Mrs Chandles would have done. I was afraid. Mrs Chandles had such ideas about people and money that I was afraid. And I did not hand up the dollar that evening nor the next evening nor the one after that. And on the following one I went under the house and put the dollar on one of those little ledges between rafter and floor. And I left it there, trying to think out a good excuse, and waiting for a favourable time when I could go up to Mrs Chandles with it.

TWENTY-SEVEN

There came a fine break in the weather. For a spell we began having plenty of sun and little rain and people were saying the Indian Summer was here. But it could not be. Mr Langley said this. Mr Langley said the time of the Indian Summer was long past. But the rains held up, anyhow. It was as if the clouds had drained themselves out and hung there sadly because they could not rain any more.

Once again every morning was market morning for me. And the

market was very colourful now with the fruit of the season. For one thing the melons were at their largest. But these days they were not so delicious for they had had too much water and there was not the dry sweetness that I knew. But the first mangoes of the season were sweeter than any mangoes I had had and they smelt strongly and the whole market reeked with them. There were oranges and tamarinds too and the large mauvish sapodillas, and indeed there was nothing more delicious than sapodillas in or out of season. I went to the stalls with the experience of months behind me and I got good value, and there was still good over-money, and when I got tired of one fruit, I tried another. I never tired of sapodillas. Even now in the market there was a little of the green corn, and people could not have enough of that, and the market floor was always untidy with the husk of corn. For Mrs Chandles, there was the best melongenes to go with beef, and there was not the small round cucumbers but the long one, and there were plenty of shalots and roucous for seasoning. And Mrs Chandles was lucky again, for this was the season of the yams.

The vendors knew me well by now, and they could almost tell what things I came for, and how much I wanted, and the things Mrs Chandles liked best. It astonished me and pleased me very much that they should know this. Every morning I bought things off the Indian women with the channa stalls, and if I asked for barah and channa they would laugh and pour on just the amount of pepper I liked with it, and if I bought something else they were sure to give me overweight. They would hold the balance scales high, and if it was cush-cush I was buying, they would put the weight in one balance and the cush-cush in the other, and they would put so much cush-cush as to tip the balance by far. They laughed all the time and they talked in Hindu to one another and they looked very nice in their saris and muslin veils. And mostly there would be gold-plated teeth in their mouths and heavy gold bracelets on their wrists and ankles. They were very pleasant to buy from.

Whenever they spoke in English it would be to ask me about Brinetta and I would say I did not know where Brinetta was. 'Where she garn,' they would press, 'you don't know where she garn?' And when I said no, they would shake their heads and look at each other as if to say it was very strange I did not know. They had never forgotten Brinetta.

These days I liked the market especially for the boiled corn.

These cobs were the last of the crop and somehow they were more suitable for boiling. Very few were roasted now. At the stall I would pay my four cents and I would peep over into the cooking-oil tin and when the vendor surfaced two or three with the big spoon I would say which one I wanted. And usually she would take the corn-cob steaming hot from the cooking-oil tin and she would say, 'Careful!' and she would quickly get out some husks and put the hot yellow corn into it and hand it quickly to me. And I would sink my teeth into the steaming cob and the vendor would laugh at this and she would tell the other vendors about me. They all knew about me, about how I liked corn.

Sometimes, while buying, I would be engrossed in the things the vendors said among themselves. They talked about the weather and their own produce. They said this was not the weather for tomatoes at all, but it was first-class for yams, and you could see that those who grew yams were jubilant. These would be having a big season this year. They talked about the season for planting peas, especially bodi and pigeon peas, and they feared very much about the weather going wrong. They had many ideas about the season.

The rain, it seemed, had been a little too much for the dasheen and the eddoes, but some of them said, What would happen to the cassava if plenty rain didn't fall? And what would happen to the yam? Those were the vendors who sold cassavas and yams and indeed, the casavas were very long on their stalls, and people stopped and bought of these and said to the vendors the cassava was eating well. This made the vendors very proud. You could see they were not glad of this new bright weather. I felt they were praying for more rain. And of course plenty more rain would fall. And things like cassavas and yams – vegetables that liked water – would flourish. The Lisbon yams, too, were at their best, and Mrs Chandles was cheerful about them, and often she would say to me, at lunch, 'You bought this yam from the same feller?' and when I said yes, she would say, 'Tell him the yam eating good.' When Mrs Chandles said things like that, she was really pleased.

The changes around the fish stalls were different. The price of red-fish had gone up. The small heaps there used to be were even smaller now. The fish-vendors said the rains were hampering the fishing. But the cocro fish was plentiful and cheap. The cocro came out to feed after the rains and they caught nets-full of them. But if at home I suggested the cocro – which was a carrion-fish – Mrs Chandles' stomach would be delicate all day. Red-fish was so expensive but for Mrs Chandles it was the only decent fish of the sea. So we paid the high price for it. But apart from the matter of fish, the market flourished with cheap, good things, and on mornings – especially Saturday mornings – it was jam-packed with the crowds of the town.

Now, too, the town had taken on a new liveliness of colour. That is, apart from the colour of the flowers in the verandas. There was the vivid green of the big trees – the coconut, the mango, the great cedar – and also the green of the hedges, lush with hibiscus, the red hibiscus flowers over-hanging the pavements. And there was the yellow-leafed pommecette, all about the town, and yet looking as out-of-place here as was the great cedar. All the yards were grassy, too – where there was not concrete – and in the open spaces the greenness of the grass was almost startling. And all this green, along with the strong, vivid one of the mountain-top when the mist lifted – all this green blended sharply with the yellowness of the sun, and with the flowers, and with the red roofs of the houses.

I remembered walking through the short-cut in the heat of the dry season when the tall trees among the houses had been stricken and barren-looking, and had not caught my eye at all. I remembered seeing the mango – so sensitive to heat – and their leaves had been shrivelled up and their barks peeled, as if they had surrendered and could take no more. I remembered the cedar, too, one of the giant cedars, and I had even looked at it and thought how much firewood there was here. But all these trees had sprung to life again, with the rains, and were so rich in leaf now, it was unbelievable. But I had seen this myself. And now I watched the great cedars sending even more branches into the sky of the town.

I had become even more fascinated with Mount Naparaima. I had watched it from the dry season to the wet and I had seen it change slowly and now there were no more open spaces and the whole crown seemed more violently overgrown with trees. In the moments of the sun its outline was sharp and clear-cut, but when the sky grew overcast, it stood dark and forbidding, its head clouded in mist. Sometimes I watched it almost all the way from the market. And I often wondered if people still picnicked up there, and if they did, where did they sit down to picnic up there.

These days Julia kept coming to my mind whenever I was on my way from the market. I had not seen her for a long time now, since the height of the rainy season. When I left the short-cut I usually walked slowly in Cascade Street. I did that most days without once seeing Julia and then one day I made up my mind and went straight to the house to see her.

'Well, well! Franco!' she said, on seeing me. 'Well, what's cooking, boy?'

I said I was well. I said I had come to see if she could lend me a book.

'Okay, come in, man, come and take what you want.'

She led me to the little place where the case of books was. It was half dining-room and half sitting-room and it was darkened by closed windows. There were so many things here that we could hardly turn about without colliding and I enjoyed colliding with Julia. Julia's mother didn't seem to have risen yet but her sister, fat-faced Enid, passed backward and forward through the room. Enid's face was friendly to me and it grinned widely at me whenever she passed through. I looked at some of the books I had not seen before and I glanced through the first few pages to see if they would be nice to read. Enid passed again and she stopped and whispered something to Julia.

'Yes,' Julia said, 'I was noticing that.'

I looked up, knowing they were talking about me. Enid went on her way. 'Any book you like?' Julia said. 'Enid say you getting big man now.'

Enid passed back and she looked at me again up and down and it seemed she was really surprised at how I had grown. Every time she had passed she was a little different. The first time she had had curlers in her hair, and then she had hurried out with her hair all loose and flowing, and then she had rushed out again and back with a half-buttoned bodice and a kettle. Now she was speaking to Julia again but not in a whisper.

'Just give him six months time and bet we'll have to watch out!'

This greatly amused Julia and embarrassed me very much. And after a while Julia left the room saying to me, stay and look for what book I wanted, she had to get ready to go out. She came out presently with the same kettle Enid had had, and she had one hand hurriedly loosening out her plaits as she went into the kitchen.

'Okay, I'll take this one,' I said. I had really come to see her, not to borrow any book.

'Right, then,' she said, 'well I'll see you.' And seeing that I hesitated, she said, 'Oh, you want to tell your girl-friend good-bye?' And she called, 'Enid! Een-id!'

'No,' I said, but she still called. I was confused and laughing and

I went down the steps. But when I reached out in the road Enid was standing leaning over the veranda. She was grinning and looking at me.

'So long, Franco,' she said.

'So long.'

I hurried away and made for Romaine Street.

I pictured her again as she had just been, leaning over in the veranda there, telling me, 'So long.' Her hair had been already plaited and she looked very like Julia. Only that she was much younger. She was still a pupil. She was one of the big girls at Julia's old school. She had big eyes and her cheeks looked so juicy and Julia had said I wanted to tell my girl-friend good-bye. That made me laugh again and then I fixed my face for people would see I was laughing to myself. I wondered if when I called there again Julia would be so silly and would say the same thing again. And I wondered if Enid would pass up and down again with that half buttoned bodice and if she would come out into the veranda when I was going and say, So long, again. I was occupied with this the whole time. I was occupied with this when I opened our gate and passed underneath the house and went up the backsteps into the house.

TWENTY-EIGHT

The so-called Indian Summer finished. After the few weeks of the sun, the rains came down again as furiously as before. And now here was the real season of the thunder, and the sudden deathly cracks seemed to tear the earth. And here was the season of the lightning too – the forked lightning that flashed and remained for seconds circling the sky. And if I was at home at such a time and it was evening I would be sitting at the dining-room table with my head in my arms, listening to the lashing of the water on the roof, and to the overflowing splashes from the spoutings on to the concrete below, and I would be thinking of all sorts of things – of Julia and Enid, of Brinetta, of how the market was going now, and about the town, and about the rain.

October was past and so was a short school holiday that had come with it. Not much had happened during that space. There was a little sun and I had stolen chances to play in the yard of the next-door school. But usually the sky had been overcast and there had always been the feeling that the bright spell would not last. And indeed it hadn't.

These days I did not have to get up for market. Mrs Chandles did not have to ask how heavily the rains were falling. Whenever the rains passed a little I was sent out to the Coffee Street for groceries, and it was there, one evening, that I had heard people talking of the floods. Floods had taken place in the near villages.

Bridges had been swept away and houses had water come through the windows, and elderly people talking about it, said it was the wrath of God on the place. I was sorry Mrs Chandles never bought newspapers for I could read newspapers and would have known all about it myself. But although Mrs Chandles said all newspapers were liars I had the feeling that these floods had happened because the rains had fallen very hard.

It was difficult enough to get to school on mornings. But I always went, using an old jacket against the weather. This was the same jacket Barrington's father had lent me. Barrington talked about this at school. The classes were usually a quarter full now, and so there was little work doing, and being in high spirits because of the weather outside, there was much fun throughout the day.

Miss Tomlin seldom came now to find out about the noise. Perhaps she had become used to it. But anyway it was not easy to hear other noises with such a clatter on the roofs above. Such days were chilly and those of us that were present sat together at one desk and we huddled up against each other and Learie drew things in his copybooks and made us laugh.

Only once did Mr Soames catch us like this. He seemed to have stolen quietly into the class and he had us all surprised looking up and seeing him standing there in front the class. The worst surprise had been Mr Langley's. He jerked up stiffly, his eyes shining, and he said, 'Sir,' and we all could see he had got a shock from not expecting Mr Soames. It was so still in the class then you could almost hear the sound that every drop of rain made. Mr Soames looked outside at the greyness of the day and all he said was that the weather was not good. Then he went away. After that Mr Langley was cross all afternoon and Learie drew a picture of how he had looked when Mr Soames had stepped in. We burst out laughing and Learie tore up the picture and Mr Langley said, 'Boys! Boys!' and we were afraid afterwards that Mr Soames might come back.

For there were other times when he had come in and if there was even the suspicion of bad behaviour, he would ask Mr Langley which of the boys were the stubborn ones. He would say, 'Show me the bad boys! I want to have a chat with the stubborn boys!' And at such times I would hold myself tight and tense afraid that I might be pointed out. No tension would be more killing than the tension of those few moments, and you could feel it lift away and get free again when Mr Soames went away with the stubborn boys.

And usually after they were gone the rest of the class would get work to do for the first time of the day. It might be sums on the blackboard. Mr Langley would write them down and then look at them from a distance and we would find them very hard and Mr Langley would say, well try them, it wouldn't matter if we got them wrong. That would put us easy again.

On the wall over Mr Langley's table there was a rather large calendar. I always looked at it, noticing the picture of the Chinese girl and looking at the Chinese writing and at the Sundays printed in red figures. I had often, with a great thrill, watched Mr Langley peel off the months. Some time ago he had peeled off September, and lately it was October that went, and now my heart beat anxiously every time I watched November on the wall.

Most of the boys knew I was going home for Christmas. On the calendar there was an ink-mark ticking off the number fifteen and I knew it was thirty days between now and home. I had been counting the days for quite some time now. I had thought of that every evening while going home. Learie and I were not good friends any more because of the dollar I had not spent with him, but even he knew, and he told other boys I was going away for Christmas. That made me very glad and in a way I wished I had spent the dollar and been good friends with him. It was only when my mind ran on this that I remembered Edwin's money on the ledge.

I had told Mrs Princet, too, that I was going home. Mrs Chandles had sent me over there and I had said to her I was going to my Ma for Christmas. Her face had lit up and she had said, 'You don't say!' And she had asked if I would be staying for New Year's too or if I'd be coming back before then. I had not thought of that and I told her I had not thought of it and I did not know.

She said well New Year's day was a big day in the country. She said it would be a shame for me to go home and have to come back before that. She said anyway if I was here for New Year's I must remember the regatta on the wharf.

Yes, the regatta. I had heard quite a lot about the New Year's day regatta. When I had first started school here, in January, it had been still fresh in mind, and it was the favourite topic in the class. They had talked about the swimming races, and they had said Quammie was the giant, Quammie was better than anybody in the South. And they had talked about the launch-rides. The rides were four cents a time and the launches went right round Farellon and back. Farellon was the big rock far out with the concrete house upon it. When I had been on the wharf I had forgotten to see if I could spot it, but indeed the boys had always talked about it when they talked about the launch rides. They had talked about the rides and about Quammie every single day.

But I did not want to come back for the regatta, really. At Mayaro there were many things, too, on New Year's day. For one thing, sports on the beach. And the fair at our own R.C. School. But even without these things I would prefer to stay at home till New Year's and come back afterwards. Because it was a whole week between Christmas and New Year's. A whole week at home with Anna and Sil and Felix, playing cricket and all sorts of things, and I wondered what would Anna and Felix and Sil say when they saw me.

Perhaps they would say, like Enid, that I had got big. I knew I had. I could feel it. Then, too, all my pants were now too short for me. They held me very tight at the seat. I got teased about this at school. Perhaps the first thing they would say at home was that my pants were tight. Perhaps they had grown, too.

It was easy for me to picture what they would say when I first arrived. I would want to play cricket right away, though. Perhaps they would think they could get me out easily. These fellers here could bowl harder than Sil and Felix and I still made runs against them. I wondered if Cyril would be there while I was batting in the savannah and afterwards maybe he would want to give me a job when I left school. Sil and Felix wouldn't get me out so quickly. Not with those hop-and-drop balls. But Ma might chase us from the sun. I wondered if Ma would chase us from the sun.

I had told Mrs Princet I would like it if I could stay for New Year's at Mayaro. She said, well, why didn't I ask Mr Chandles. I could see she did not like talking about Mr Chandles, because her face, always so bright, had changed then. I said, I would ask him. She had said, anyway if I had to come back I could always spend New Year's on the wharf. She had said the regatta was a big thing. Fête for so! she'd said.

I had been very much cheered up by Mrs Princet. Also by the sweet-bread I had been taking back home. There had been one for me in the bag. I had walked back fast, wondering all the time if I could find out about whether I could stay at home over the New Year's holiday. I thought I would ask Mr Chandles when he came home but I was a little afraid. I was afraid he might think, since I had got an inch and wanted a mile I'd better stay here altogether. I didn't quite know what to do. I didn't want to take any chances with my going home. But Mr Chandles wasn't bad these days. Anyway, I would ask the old lady first and hear what she said.

TWENTY-NINE

December had hardly started when Mrs Chandles, venturing outside, slipped and fell. Why in the name of heaven she went outside I did not know. She had not liked the sun and preferred the rains, but with the new brightness she had been as excited as a child. For the rainy season had been draining off now and the skies clearing up, and many people thinking back, said the rains had not been 'much of a muchness'. They said that it was a good thing that San Fernando was so hilly and that the water always ran off. Yet they had feared about floods.

But all that was past now. And I could see the excitement in them, for the sun. And that was very natural, to me, for I had felt the same way. But I was surprised to find this in Mrs Chandles because I had understood it was the sun she feared. And now she had come outside on the slippery drying ground and she had slipped and fallen and I had had to help her up the stairs and she had been in great agony. She had been taken straight to bed and was still there.

She seemed to be suffering a great deal. The doctor who had come over said she had damaged some pelvis or something and he had said she caught a chill. I was very much afraid for her at first. I was afraid, too, that if she got worse Mr Chandles would not let me go to Mayaro any more. But the doctor had said she wasn't all that bad. And he had winked at me but I had known Mrs Chandles wasn't putting on anything.

When the doctor had rung Mr Chandles and he had come home that midweek evening he had asked me what the hell Mrs Chandles had been doing outside. I said I didn't know. He said it was damned right silly. This surprised me and I turned away because I thought he was very vexed. And yet he spoke kindly to me. He said the rains were going away now, thank goodness. He turned up his chin indicating Mrs Chandles' room and he said, 'You know what that mean now? That mean I have to take some kind of leave from the damn job.' I said, 'Oh,' and then I asked him if Mrs Chandles was *that* sick. 'It look so,' he said. And I asked him directly if I was still going home for Christmas. He said, 'Why not?' I said, 'Well—' He said, 'Hell!' And seeing that I didn't laugh right away, he said, 'Oh well, yes, you'd be going to see your old lady just the same.' I felt madly glad. Glad, too, to hear him talk like this. I felt he was in good spirit, even though Mrs Chandles was sick. He talked of going to Carib Street to see someone to ask her to look after Mrs Chandles for a while. I asked him directly if I could stay at Mayaro over the New Year's. He thought for a little and then he said, 'Why not?' He asked did I like any regatta. I said, yes, and there was regatta in Mayaro on New Year's Day. He looked at me sharply and I remembered he had known Mayaro and I said, 'Oh, I meant school sports, not regatta.' He said, if I wanted I could stay for New Year's. And I could travel back the day after. I felt this was fine. I felt it was really very good. I didn't want to be overjoyed, but gratefulness had welled up inside me. Mr Chandles said he'd better go now to see the lady on Carib Street. From where we were, just in front of the kitchen, Mrs Chandles' occasional groan came to us. I knew Mrs Chandles wasn't putting on anything. Even when her legs had given so much trouble before, she had not groaned, so to give the feeling she was all right. She was far from all right now. I wondered if she was very bad. I wondered if Mr Chandles still hated her much.

I was feeling in good spirit. Mr Chandles had gone into his bedroom. He had gone into Mrs Chandles' room first but I had not heard if any words passed between them. I had already done the little chores in the kitchen, and I thought, what else was there to do? I could not think of anything. About a week ago Mr Chandles had brought a pair of ducks, and I had already fed these. They liked the left-over bread and I had given them that, throwing bits to different parts of the coop, and I had taken an old sardine can, wrung the cover off, and filled it with water and had given them water in that. Mr Chandles had come downstairs to see them and he had noticed what I had done and was surprised and he had asked where had I fed ducks before. I knew about ducks because Ma had fed the Forestry's ducks. I had been very pleased with myself.

I went to the back steps which I always came to when there was something happening. I sat on the top step looking across at Celesta Street. There was much wind. There was a little sharpness in the air, as was customary with a December evening, and there was the feeling of Christmas over the town. The curtains blew out like sails in the open windows and then they were blown up showing the insides of the houses, and in the house directly before me a woman came and pulled the curtain ends back inside and she stayed a little while doing something to them and when she left the curtain did not blow out any more.

I saw the big mango tree rustling in the wind. It was just a little way up Celesta Street and I had seen it half-dead in the dry season and I knew it was mango but did not know what kind. Then when the rains began no one had to tell me what kind of mango it was. Even before the yellow-gold blossoms came out I knew. By the long dark-green leaves I could have told anyone it was rose-mango and I could have said that this was the sweet mango with the sour seed. The humming-birds had pestered the blossoms as they had pestered all blossoms and I was glad when the dried flowers blew away leaving little green mangoes on the tree. I could not have seen the mangoes from here until they were weeks old, for they were of the same shade of green as the leaves. I had watched them from then onwards until with watering mouth I had seen the fruit grow yellow then ripe-red and at times with pain I had seen people who had never watched them from the time they were small come with long bamboo rods picking them, and sometimes even climbing the tree to get the big ripe ones. And mostly on an early morning I had seen the rosy, dropped fruit on the ground. But all that was gone now. The mango season was over. I watched the wind

113

rustling the leaves very hard and every now and then a dried leaf would blow off, sailing between the houses and then getting lost to my view. And then I looked at the very tall coconut tree far in the distance and there too the wind was very high.

It suddenly occurred to me that I was hearing some sort of sound and then I realized that it was the radio playing. Radio music was a very unusual thing in this house. It was playing very softly, very low. I wondered, was Mr Chandles back. I did not hear him come in. If he was back he must have walked in very quietly. It was even stranger to think of him walking quietly. I felt a sort of inner amusement. Not the sort of amusement to make me laugh aloud. I got up from the patch of sun and went down into the yard. I could not see anyone in the school-yard but I had just heard voices over there. The blueness of sky around the coconut tree was a bigger blueness now. Presently I heard the voices again and two boys came running around the other side of the school. They were trying to put a kite up. This made me interested right away. Of course it was December. The kite season already! Well, January was the kite season. Still . . .

The boys ran up and down along the flat place beside the school. The bigger boy was in front holding the reel of thread and the small one was trying to give a lag. But the kite would not go up at all. I laughed. Every now and again the big boy came and examined the kite and he was in a bad temper with the smaller boy because the kite wouldn't go up. But the reason was not the smaller boy at all. Anybody could see that the tail wasn't enough. If you had a Mad Bull kite you had to give it plenty of tail. The thread, I could see, was all right, but they had to put on plenty more tail. They could even put two long strips. They stood on the pavement side, the smaller boy standing on the pavement itself to give more height, and they both were at the ready and then the bigger boy cried 'Now!' and the smaller one let go and the other came running backwards into the wind. I didn't want to shout out to him because now the place had to be very quiet, with Mrs Chandles sick, and in any case Mr Chandles might be inside. I made a sign to attract him – the bigger boy – and when he watched I made him a sign to say the tail was far too short. I then pulled my right hand vigorously along my outstretched left arm up to the shoulder, showing that the tail had to be at least so long. But they could not understand. I put my hands beside my mouth and I said, 'Tail!' 'What?' they shouted. I made them the sign meaning, Come over here.

I took the kite in my hand. It was such a strong well-made kite, it was a pity they did not know about it. The ribs were big and strong. They were made of strip bamboo. Those were the sort of ribs for a Mad Bull kite. This had the right quality paper too and real Mad Bull colours. It was a pity these fellers couldn't appreciate it. If you had a Mad Bull you had to know how to fly it. It didn't take any fool to fly a Mad Bull. I held the kite out before me picturing it up there playing with the clouds. When it was up there you had to know how to hold it. You couldn't give too much twine at first unless the wind was in your favour. These little fellers were really too light to fly a Mad Bull properly. I could imagine the Mad Bull wanting to go and *they* trying to hold it back. I wanted to laugh. Anyway this was a first-class kite. The feller who made this knew about making kites.

'Who make this kite?' I said.

'Uncle,' the smaller one said. I supposed the bigger one wanted to say *he* made it.

'You have a master kite,' I said.

I couldn't think of any rags indoors that I could tear a tail from. There was a piece of my bedding, though, that should make a good tail. I didn't want to go inside to do that if Mr Chandles was in.

I couldn't help laughing at the ridiculous little piece of tail they had tied on. It was a miracle how the kite hadn't nose-dived on the yard and got broken up. I turned to the bigger boy. He was only a little smaller than me but he had no kite-sense. 'Listen,' I said, 'you want plenty more tail here. For this to go up you want tail all this—' I had stretched out both my arms to show him the length. 'All that,' I said.

If you hadn't very heavy tail, that was the length to put. When Felix made Mad Bulls that was what he put. You could tie on a zwill, too, if you wanted. A razor blade would be a good zwill for this one. If you had a new razor blade, and you were a good kite-man it wouldn't take a minute to cut any twine cleanly and send the other kite flying across the village. I wondered if anybody would cut this kite down. I had the sneaking feeling that this kite wouldn't last. I could picture a good kite-man fixing on a sharp zwill then sending up his kite to have a few words with this one. I couldn't talk for laughing. 'You putting a zwill?' I said. 'What?' the bigger one said. 'Okay,' I said, 'Okay, don't worry!' They were laughing heartily too though they couldn't tell what I was laughing about. 'Go and get a good strong tail,' I said. 'Ask your uncle.'

I kept them just a minute longer while I loosened the compass, pulled it down a little and drew it tight, then I gave the kite back to them. They ran out and across the street, excited. I didn't know all that much about kites but I was a professor compared to those two. They knew absolutely nothing. They were out of view now. I looked at Celesta Street a little. Evening was closing in and yet I was feeling the hotness of the sun on my head. I went up into the passage to listen to see if Mrs Chandles was still groaning. Then I came back to have a look at the ducks.

At about six o'clock I went in to get Mrs Chandles' porridge ready. There was no sound from the radio now. I did not go into the drawing-room to see if Mr Chandles was in because I knew he was or the radio would not have been playing. In the kitchen, I lit the stove and put on the aluminium pot, half full with water. That was just enough to make Mrs Chandles' cream-of-wheat. Usually I almost filled the pot with water, and so what porridge remained after Mrs Chandles' was mine. I was feeling filled-up and I didn't want to drink anything this evening. I turned the fire low and then I went and leaned over the window looking out.

The water was simmering and I looked at it but it was not boiling yet. It was making tiny bubbles around the rim of the pot and I knew it would soon be boiling. I measured out the cream-of-wheat in a tea-cup and then I poured hot water into the cup so the flakes would soak. When the water began boiling I poured what was in the tea-cup into the pot and using a spoon I scraped in whatever flakes had stuck in the cup. Then I covered the pot and stood there and peeped in every second to see if the porridge was beginning to rise. Presently it lifted the cover and spilled all over the stove before I could turn the fire off.

I wiped off the stove leaving the pot open meanwhile so the porridge would cool. Somehow I was not angry about the boil-over. The brightness of fading day, the thoughts of Christmas coming, and the thoughts of my going home, were all seeming to run around inside me. Even the boys with the kite had stirred me up a bit. The feeling was pleasantly strange. It seemed to be within my whole body. Julia, too, came to my mind now. Julia was kind and she was very pretty. I wondered about Enid. Julia was a big girl and very nice.

The Christmas feeling seemed to be there even though my mind flitted to different things. I kept thinking of Julia and then I thought of Mayaro again and I tried to picture how it would be

116

when I arrived in the bus at the junction by Chin Hong's shop. I knew there would be people standing around there because people always stood there just to see who arrived. This sent my mind wilder and more excited and I wondered, would it be Edgill driving, and Balgobin, again? Balgobin would be surprised and would pretend not to see me at first and would look outside and say, 'Cheese and Ages!' and I wouldn't be able to talk, for laughing.

I jumped quickly from my thoughts, and for the moment I was confused, forgetting what I was meaning to do. Mr Chandles walked into the kitchen. I moved away from the sink and he went straight to it and was washing his hands. He had towel and soap and the soap perfumed the kitchen. I said I had the porridge ready and was going to take it in.

He didn't seem to hear. He had closed the tap and his head was stuck right out of the window looking up at the sky. 'Sun still out, eh?' he said. His voice was very pleasant and as he turned round his face was pleasant too. When his face was pleasant it always surprised me at first. I was very relieved and then I was feeling glad.

'Yes,' I said.

'Yes,' he said, shaking his head contemplatively, 'and just now is Christmas, too.'

'Yes.'

And then, as if suddenly remembering, he said he had got the lady to come to look after Mrs Chandles.

It was a good thing. I tried to look as though I felt he was very kind. And then he said, 'By the time you go home and come back here'll be all changed up, boy.'

I had put in the condensed milk and now I was going to put the sugar in. What would be changed up, except that Mrs Chandles might be worse? Except that it would be a new year? A new year was a big thing. If—

'You know Miss Samuels coming?'

My heart gave a big jump inside. That was Marva. What was this all about? I had stopped with the spoonful of sugar about to be poured into the porridge and I could not remember if I had put in a spoonful before or not.

'Marva?' I said.

'Don't tell me you don't know we getting married for Christmas? Mother didn't tell you?'

I had directly put the sugar into the porridge and I was stirring

117

it. I did not know they were getting married for Christmas. Nor did Mrs Chandles, I was sure. Last year Ma had kept talking about it and had kept saying, 'Next year,' but I had gone through the whole year without thinking of their getting married at all. Then too, they were supposed to be going down to the Great Asphalt area in La Brea, not coming to live here. I put the condensed milk and the sugar bottle back into the safe. I could actually hear how my heart was racing inside.

'Surprised?' Mr Chandles laughed. 'Yes, she'll be here. Mr Chandles turning over a new leaf, boy. Everything will be settled down next year.'

'Yes,' I said, and I smiled because I knew he wanted me to. I roused myself and took out the pile of saucers from the top of the safe and I tried to rest them on the kitchen dresser, and they rattled together with the trembling of my hands. I was not feeling dismayed or anything. In fact I was feeling very different. My mind was now very clear although there was this nervousness. I had taken out the saucer with the border of blue rings and had put the little pile back. And now I rested the cup of porridge in the saucer, and walking carefully, watching the trembling of my hands and trying hard to stop it, I went to Mrs Chandles' door and knocked.

'Yes,' she said weakly. It seemed to take a lot from her to say, 'yes'.

I went in.

'What's the time now?' she said. Her voice was not above a whisper and her face seemed already drawn. She tried to sit up, and at the end of it she was half-sitting, half-lying back against the pillow. She seemed to have been in great pain. Already, she looked so stricken, I could hardly believe it.

I told her what the time was. She didn't say anything. I didn't know why on earth she wanted to know the time. Maybe she was waiting on this person who was coming to look after her. She didn't seem to be paying any mind to the porridge. I drew a chair near the bed and rested the saucer with cup upon it.

'Fever,' Mrs Chandles said, 'roasting fever.'

Her eyes were red and watery-looking. She was so weak that she had to fix herself plumb before stretching for the cup. When I saw it was that she was doing I handed the cup to her. I was afraid she would spill everything. She had ague too but she didn't say so. She gave the cup back to me and she whispered something. I didn't hear what she said but I got it the second time and resting the porridge down I went around the chair and put my hands across her back supporting her and I brought the pillow up nearer to the rails of the bed, and I let her ease back on it and she was a lot more comfortable now. I gave her the cup again.

'The lady coming?' she said.

'Yes. I think so.'

'When?'

'Any time now.'

'What about Edwin?'

'I don't know.'

'Anybody tell him?'

'I don't know, Mrs Chandles.' She looked so frustrated that I said I would ask.

'No, no,' she said. 'It's orright. Leave it.'

Within these few days she had grown very ill. It was a sudden change. True, she had got a bad fall, but although the doctor had said she was not to get out of bed, she had still been able to limp down to get what she wanted. But since she had taken worse she could hardly turn on the bed of her own effort, and now, looking at her there, it struck me that when the doctor had telephoned Mr Chandles the second time and said she was critical he had been serious about it. I forgot Marva for the moment. I was feeling bewildered. I was feeling sick too. I had not been in the bedroom since the doctor had called today and I did not see him going out but I wondered what he felt now to see Mrs Chandles like this. She couldn't be pretending now.

'The thing's getting cold,' I said.

I did not expect her to take it but she said, 'Lift me up first. Let me sit up.'

She had relaxed on the pillow and had slid down a little. I went round the chair again and supported her back and raised the pillow up to prop her. It was not difficult to do that and I was surprised to see how light she felt. Just about a week in bed and she was like a feather. And her cheekbones seemed to stick out in the skin of her face.

She was trying to drink up the porridge now. She took it in very little sips and I could see she was pressing herself to drink it. Outside the window the dusk had taken over. I could hardly see the school through the glass.

Mrs Chandles began groaning and I looked round quickly from the window. Nothing was happening except that she had stopped drinking and she was groaning and she was wanting me to take the cup from her. She had drunk a fair bit. She handed the saucer first and then she put the cup down in it spilling what was left and all but smashing the saucer. I looked round for a piece of rag to wipe up what was spilled on the edge of the bed and on the chair. 'Linden there? Call Linden. Quick!' she said. And before I could move she vomited all over the place.

THIRTY

Mrs. Chandles' strength drained badly during the following week and she could hardly do anything at all now unless somebody was there. The lady Mr Chandles brought to look after her was quite elderly too, and though she was not unwilling she was very gloomy about the situation. She looked Mrs Chandles up and down before ever touching her, and often, in front of the very sick, she made dark prophecies concerning how long all this would carry on for. She did not think Mrs Chandles had long to go again. If Mrs Chandles ever heard these things she showed no sign of taking notice. But I felt she was too sick to understand anything or even to be afraid. She lay there groaning all the time and whenever her food came back from her stomach blood came up with it. The elderly lady saw this as a very decisive sign and she said if Mrs Chandles went another month she'd eat her hat. This kind of talk, and the sight of Mrs Chandles slowly stiffening on the bed, and the prospect of death in the house, and the thought of Marva coming, terrified me.

The elderly lady seemed right. Mrs Chandles was far gone and even the doctor couldn't do anything for her now. He was very frank and he said he could not do any more at this stage. Nor could the elderly lady. Nor could anybody. There were moments when I had heard her groaning in the night, or vomiting, and I wished somebody could do something. Not because she was disturbing me. I couldn't sleep anyway. Nor was it because I loved her so much, although I felt well towards her now. It was just because I had seen what was coming and I didn't want anybody to die and I was afraid of death in the house. And perhaps I would miss Mrs Chandles a little. I was afraid of something else, too. I was afraid of Marva coming here. Things were working right for her. When the funeral moved out she would move in. Many nights I had lain in bed trying to think out why I disliked Marva so much. Many nights I lay trying to find out why I could not stay in this house one moment if Marva came here. I knew I would never give her the privilege of bossing me around. Yet that evening when Mr Chandles had spoken and when my brains had become clear I had not gone into any desperation. When I had written home I had just said frankly how things were and I had not been desperate or anything. I hadn't even said much about the old lady. I had merely said she was going to die. There was no need for me to have any panic-feelings over Marva. Everything was going to be all right. I was already fixed to go home for Christmas. Yet I was worrying so I couldn't sleep. That was silly. Mr Langley had repeatedly said: 'Everything comes to those who wait.'

By mid-December, with school having closed for Christmas, I spent the holidays being busy in the house. Mrs Chandles was – as the elderly lady said – just awaiting sentence, though I couldn't think what greater sentence could come to her now. But she was waiting all right. It was strange how hard and untiring the elderly lady worked. For, as she said herself, all she was doing was in vain. I watched her rush in and out of the room, always with hot water on the fire, always with foul-smelling bedclothes to wash. And yet she did everything with zest. It was as if she was just getting the feel of the wrestle with death and was enjoying it. I thought maybe she had always been at the side of the dying. I thought maybe it made no difference to her if death won all the time. Mostly, I wondered how was she really feeling inside, and sometimes I thought to myself how much money could Mr Chandles be paying her.

The days ran out and what at first had struck me as cold-bloodedness in the elderly lady must have been something else. Anyway if it had been that, where it disappeared to now I did not know. Mrs Chandles was as weak as she would ever be. There was plenty to do in the house and I did a little and I did not know how the elderly lady kept up. Mrs Chandles was nursed with very tender care. But it did not keep her from sinking lower with each

121

new day. And yet all that seemed to matter to the elderly lady was to keep Mrs Chandles from the grave. That was how things looked to me. The doctor came always but you couldn't look to him for any hope. Sometimes I thought maybe he was a good man because he didn't want to make you hope in vain. He must have seen the old lady hadn't a chance whatever. Often when he arrived I walked behind him to hear what he would say after he entered the room. At first he only used to stare at Mrs Chandles lying there on the bed. Now the first thing he did when he saw her was to look at the elderly lady and shake his head. The elderly lady would reply by pouting out her lips in the way elderly people said, 'What to do!' But looking at her about the house you would never think she had given up. Sometimes she called me to help her with Mrs Chandles and there was never anything like dismay in her voice. Whenever we were too slow and Mrs Chandles soiled up the sheets, all she would say was, 'Look out!' after it had already happened. This amused me. Immediately she would clean the helpless sick, and getting me to help, she would hold Mrs Chandles to one side of the bed, then to the other, and like that she would put new, clean sheets on the bed. Holding Mrs Chandles was no strain for my arms and she felt like just skin and bones. Anyway after putting on the clean sheets the dirty linen would be bundled into a cardboard box to be taken downstairs to wash. But before this was done Mrs Chandles would be put to lie nice and comfortable on the bed.

At such times I had always tried to do what I had to do without thinking of the sick before me. For her eyes would be like death itself and her body would be as stiff as board though it did not seem this was on her account. Usually she never seemed to know what was going on. And sometimes while I held her there amidst all the mess I felt as though the stench of the bedclothes was going to suffocate me.

And so looking on at these things I knew the end could not be far off now. I had seen only one dead person before, and thinking of that face now, and of this, it was striking how alike were the faces of death. I had gone to the house and had watched that dead man's face and was terrified. I had come out and had run home crying in the dark.

These days there was not much that was diverting. I went to the market only once in a while now. I went whenever there was some special food to be got for Mrs Chandles and there was no other place but the market to get it from. But on the whole I hardly left the house to go far away. There was always something to be done here. I was always needed indoors.

The elderly lady all but lived here these days. Only when Mrs Chandles was asleep on afternoons did she get a chance to go up to Carib Street. I didn't know if she had any children to look after. If she had, they were having to look after themselves now. At the times when she went away to Carib Street the house would seem so still and sombre and I would go and lean against the kitchen window, feeling all sad inside me, and I would try to liven myself up by thinking of Christmas or just noticing how hot and bright the weather had become. Not that there were never any rains now. But they were very rare. You could see very few clouds in the sky now. You knew it was no longer the time of the rains.

I managed on these occasions to forget the affairs of the house a little. If I put my mind on Christmas, which was very new now, my heart would begin to lift and then I would grow quite excited. But it was not always I could put my mind on this. Sometimes the gloom seemed to hang all around me. Christmas was so near but at moments it seemed miles away.

For weeks now, I had been seeing the signs of Christmas in the houses of Celesta Street. They had put up new curtains already. It was amazing how the curtains brightened the street. I had watched the women fasten them in the windows with much fuss. They had climbed on chairs and stretched and measured, then they had put the curtains up and fixed them, then they had taken them down again and afterwards they had stood on the chairs and measured again, and they had held up the curtains and pulled the cords and fastened them, and at last they had left them up there when they came down, and then they had walked out into the road to see from that distance how nice the curtains looked.

The curtains looked very nice. They made me think of Christmas just to watch them. Not only the curtains but the streamers and tinsels which you saw whenever the jalousies were down. The men folk who lived in those houses were very pleased. Sometimes they came in on bicycles and you saw when they looked at what had been put in the windows that they were very pleased.

Up on the Coffee Street the Christmas preparations were breathtaking. I had never seen shops and stores so gaily decorated and I had never seen such wonderful things in the shop-windows. These business places were always crammed with people these days and all along the pavements there was always a jam-session of people. I had not been out of the house for a few days but sometimes while in the veranda I heard people passing in the street, and mostly they would be talking about Christmas shopping and they would say, 'Boy! Not me and that Coffee Street. It's murder up there!' And whenever I wasn't wanted for a while I would stand outside the gate and look towards the Coffee Street to see what was happening up there.

But from Romaine Street you could see very little of what was happening there. You only saw crowds walking along at the top. If it was morning there would probably be mountain mist above the shops. The mist was one further sign that the dry season was here. Usually, on seeing this and on seeing the bushy cane-lands from the kitchen window I knew that for me there would be no more watching the cane-cutters and there would be no more bright, crackling fires in the night. I knew these things and they made me sad in some way but they never tamed my anxiety to go home. Indeed, on the still, sombre afternoons, when I leaned against the window looking out, if these thoughts of home took root in me I would stand gazing out on Celesta Street but seeing nothing but miles – nothing but the long, long miles and the far village. And often, while in this frame of mind, I would hear the front door open and the elderly lady would come hurrying in. Seeing her would bring back all the heaviness of the house upon me. She would come straight into the kitchen and she would look at me with her brows raised. And I would say, 'She still sleeping.' And she would tiptoe and go to see for herself. Usually Mrs Chandles would still be sleeping.

THIRTY-ONE

I remember that it was the Sunday just before Christmas that the house seemed full of people. Mr Chandles who had been coming home at week-ends as usual, and who had not looked too distressed about Mrs Chandles' condition, seemed a little strained now. He had arrived very early on Sunday morning and he had been very friendly to me. He had said he was on his Christmas leave from now and he would go down to the High Street by Tuesday and get me up some little things before I went home. Knowing that I was going up to a higher class in the new year he had said when I returned both of us would go to the Southern Printerie and he would buy all my school-books at once so I would have a chance to look up in them before school re-opened. And then he had said the old lady looked very low. That was how he had said it. When he said 'old lady' it made me feel he liked her somewhat. I had never heard him say it like that before.

I said, yes, she was very poorly now. When he was like this I could talk to him in a free way, as if he was more like an uncle than like himself. When I said she was very poorly a wistful smile came over his face, and he said, that would be some Christmas with a dead body in the house! And a bride in the house, too, I thought. I could think this way now because – well, because in a way I did not care.

Mr Chandles went on talking and I felt he was warm towards me. He talked about all sorts of things and about things here and there – not in a serious manner, but just by the way. I remembered he talked about the war, and there was a great victory against Rommel, the Desert Rat. He was pleased. And then we talked about the sick again. He said that girl was really a great help. He was meaning the elderly lady. He called her 'girl'. That tickled me. I liked to hear him talk like that. He seemed to be thinking of something and then he said to me, if the old lady didn't kick the bucket by Wednesday, when I came back I was sure not to see her any more. Wednesday was Christmas Eve and the day I was to travel. I said, yes. He took a glass and he filled it under the tap, and drinking it slowly, like beer, he said to me there was a lot more trouble brewing than I knew. He said I saw how he was paying the rates for the house, I was seeing for myself. He said life was a funny thing. He asked me how often Edwin came here. I said he had come a few times for this week. He asked if he and Mrs Chandles had talked a lot about the house. I reminded him that Mrs Chandles couldn't talk any more. He said, yes, yes, that was true. He looked tired. I felt he was worried and keyed-up but not depressed. He went on talking. He said trouble was brewing up but he was ready for anyone. And he said there were those who were waiting anxiously for the old lady to die.

I did not relish this conversation. I was still on Edwin's side and

I had grown to like Edwin more and more. So I turned a little now and looked out of the window. The sky was bright. Far, far away a Mad Bull shimmered and ducked, taking the wind full on.

Down in the yard the sweetbroom had pushed up so high again. I had weeded them out but it was surprising how they had pushed up so quickly. They wanted the roots pulled out, that was what. I wondered if a certain 'somebody' would pull them out when that certain 'somebody' came and was boss in this house. I doubted that very much. There were a few love-birds on the fence. I had not seen the cat for some time. Mr Chandles was still standing beside me. I didn't know if he was looking outside, too, or not. It was not really true that Edwin was waiting anxiously for Mrs Chandles to die. I knew that much. When I had gone down to the engineering works to tell him what had happened, and he came back with me and saw, he could not contain his distress. He had cried openly.

My thoughts were interrupted by Mr Chandles talking. He had been out in the dining-room and he must have seen my grip in the corner. He said I mustn't forget, get everything packed up and ready and Wednesday he would go down with me to catch the first bus. He was in a mood to talk about buses. Don't forget where to catch the Princes Town bus, he said. They were the yellow buses. Looking Mayaro way, round that traffic island. That was the Rio Claro bus he meant, at Princes Town. Anybody could tell me where to find it, he said. Ask anybody.

And then he talked about Boxing Day. That was the day he was going to get married, very quietly, no fuss at all – and it was the day Marva would be starting to live here.

'You two should do well,' he said, 'she always liked you.'

'Yes,' I said.

I did not know about weddings that were quiet and had no fuss at all. I did not know about weddings without any church-bells and without cars and without speeches and many guests. He said something like 'registry', but I didn't quite get hold of that. It was all strange to me. It sounded more like a secret than like a wedding.

I couldn't help wondering what would happen if Mrs Chandles died on Boxing Day. That would be chaos. I was sure he didn't think of that. He went on talking about the wedding. He didn't mention Mrs Samuels or anything. He said some people liked a big show. *He* liked to do things in a small way.

And then he fell silent and did not say anything for some time. And he stood there close to me and though I was looking outside I

126

had the feeling that he was worried now and had lost his composure because there was so much on his mind. I was looking outside but there was growing within me a strange, close feeling for him. It was coming home to me that at this late hour we were becoming friends. I could feel it there between us. I could feel it strong and real. When people were fooling you knew it and when they were insincere you knew it too, and you knew when they were genuine to you. Mr Chandles wasn't saying much now but he was standing there and I was standing by the window and I was feeling here was a time when he was becoming used to me, here was a time when he felt he could talk to me. I wondered when did all this start up, because it wasn't sudden. I wondered how come he felt he could talk to me like this and be friends with me. I knew he was no tyrant now and I was feeling easy with him. I looked down at the sweet-broom and at the love-birds and inside me I was feeling new.

Mr Chandles went out of the kitchen again and then I heard him in his room and then he came back into the kitchen. I felt he was walking for the sake of walking; that he did not know what to do with himself. Afterwards he slipped away again and this time by his footsteps I knew he was going into Mrs Chandles' room. When he came back into the kitchen he looked very shaken. He was looking out of the window and muttering to himself.

That same afternoon Mrs Princet arrived. She brought Winston with her. The elderly lady had fetched them chairs and they sat beside the bed watching Mrs Chandles' mouth opening and shutting. And then Edwin arrived. He walked in looking grave and looking as if he was ready for anything. There was tension immediately he came. It seemed as if the rest had known what was going on between himself and Mr Chandles and as if they were afraid something might start up. But nobody said anything. The elderly lady fetched him a chair but he preferred to stand. I went out into the kitchen and I stayed there and I, too, was afraid something might start up. But nothing happened. Nothing whatsoever. That was the Sunday just before Christmas when the house seemed full of people.

THIRTY-TWO

On Tuesday night only very little sleep came to me. I tried to sleep because the thinking of home harassed me. I was restless and uncomfortable and I turned with my face on the pillow and then with my face looking up at the ceiling again. I lay with my eyes open far into the night. I wondered how close it was getting to morning. Every few minutes I wondered that. It was painful to think of home with home so near – only hours away. With the first bus I should get there by twelve o'clock. I had worked that out. I was working that sort of thing out all the time, and I worked out how long the bus should take between every stage of the journey. I turned on my belly then on my back and I lay with my eyes open all the time. Then I closed my eyes, trying to sleep but I could not sleep, so I opened them again. I tried to shift these painful thoughts from my mind. When you were so anxious, thinking of home was very like agony. I started trying to listen to the noises coming from Mrs Chandles' room.

Mrs Princet was remaining all night at the bedside. She had come back this morning to join the elderly lady and she had decided she would stay all night. They had made a lot of coffee, to keep them awake.

Twice during the day there had been the alarm that Mrs Chandles was dead. The excitement roused her from her deep coma and when she came to she had looked enlightened and was even able to mumble something. They said she had spoken about strange places. But her tongue was very heavy and I knew they couldn't possibly gather anything.

I lay there listening to water being poured into basins and to the sounds of chairs being moved about, and to the friendly clinking of bottle on bottle, and to so many other little sounds that kept the night alive. And after some time the noises came dulled and distant and I was feeling a tiredness in my head.

Maybe it was then that I got the first patch of sleep. There seemed to have been several short patches. They were strange and more restless than my wakefulness. First I dreamed I was on the bus to Mayaro. The driver was Julia and we were hurtling along an endless white road. The bus seemed full but then it turned out we were alone on the bus. I looked at Julia without speaking and I noticed her neat cane-rowed plaits and the side of her head was very beautiful. And then she turned around to me. She was laughing. She said she could see right down inside my mind. I was appalled and tried to hide my mind. She laughed out in a vulgar way. She said: 'Little boy like you – before you study your books you studying to love big women!' Shocked and excited I had awakened from that dream.

I got up from my bedding and tip-toed out into the drawing-room. There was light in it. As I had pushed the door open the light came full and blinded me for a moment. I did not see Mr Chandles sitting in the easy chair.

'What happen?' he said.

He wasn't dressed for bed, nor was he dressed to go out. He had on pants and shirt, with no jacket on, and he wasn't wearing a tie, but had his shirt opened at the neck. As my eyes grew accustomed to the light I saw him sitting there, leaning right back, looking a bit worn.

'I just wanted to see the time,' I said.

These days I had lost all my fear for him. I knew he did not want me to fear him any more and he never shouted at me now nor talked in the old fashion. In a strange way I had begun feeling sorry for him because of the house matters but mainly because Marva was coming here.

'Time?' he now said, as if he had come back from far away. 'Look at the clock! Not even midnight yet. Take it easy!'

My disappointment in the clock was very sharp. Not even midnight yet! It seemed like ages since I'd been lying down. Good God! I thought. Mr Chandles spoke again, laughing a little. 'Go back and lie down,' he said. '*You* can't sleep and I can't sleep. Go and take a rest,' he said. 'You might drop asleep.'

I lay awake a long time after this, and then I began to feel my head a little heavy. And maybe this was when the second patch of sleep started. Immediately I was in a crowd, and I noticed the crowd was walking in procession and the procession turned out to be Mrs Chandles' funeral. I ran up to the head of the procession and there was the coffin draped and tiny borne by men in black.

And then I noticed I was not in black but in my new clothes Mr Chandles had bought. Peeping into the coffin I saw the dead face smiling and winking at me. I smiled back striving to keep up with the bearers.

And then it seemed we were not on the Coffee Street as I had thought but on the High Street. And it was not Mrs Chandles' funeral but Edwin's. And Edwin lay there with his eyes open but looking very dead. Then he spoke a word to the bearers and they turned at me crying, 'Dollar! Dollar!' I tried to break away but the crowd surrounded me and everybody seemed to be running to hold me. I cried out. The next moment my eyes were open and I was still panting.

'What happen!' Mr Chandles' voice was saying. 'Eh?' I looked up and was aware of him standing there in the dark.

'I was dreaming.'

He seemed to be giggling softly. I could see his white teeth. 'Nightmare,' he said. 'You eat too much.' I wanted to laugh too but I couldn't.

After that I sat up in bed for some time. My heart was beating very fast. There were many noises coming from the sick-room. When I felt Mr Chandles had settled down again and it was all right, I crept towards the passage and then I got up and tip-toed to the back-steps and I went underneath the house, feeling my way in the pitch-blackness. I felt my way to the concrete pillar where that certain rafter was and I passed my hand on the ledge. The dust was thick but the dollar note was there. I tried to hurry back, hitting against a pillar or two and when I reached up the stairs I almost crawled on all fours to where my grip was. I tried to open it without the smallest noise. It was not hard to do that. My grip was like any other grip except that there was no catch to fasten the cover down. I kept it closed by buckling a belt around it. I undid the belt now and I slipped the dollar right down to the bottom under all my clothes. I thought for a moment, had I put every, everything in? Yes, there was nothing else to go in. And then I remembered, and I thought, what about the clothes you have on, silly. That would have to go in, too. So I left the grip with the cover just closed but not buckled down and I crawled back and lay down quietly. I wondered how late it was now. I wondered if it was one o'clock yet. I wondered how long would it be before first cock started crowing. It might be like a whole year. It couldn't even be midnight yet. There was still light in the drawing-room. I could see it through the little space between the bottom of the door and the floor itself. I lay down.

The next thing I knew was Mr Chandles shaking me. 'Get up,' he was saying. 'Get up, boy! Get up!'

It was broad daylight.

THIRTY-THREE

I dressed nervously, feverishly. Feverish not only in haste but in thoughts. Mr Chandles was already dressed. He looked clean-shaven and in a way he looked new. He looked new in the way you saw people when you overslept on a bright morning. I was sure I was late for that first bus. Mr Chandles walked up and down from his room to the kitchen, from the kitchen to his room. He did not look impatient. I stood beside my open grip and I already had my pants on and was buttoning up my shirt. The pants were new and I was very glad of it. The shirt was new too. Mr Chandles had bought these and I was wearing the brown pants with sky-blue shirt. I felt it looked nice. But the shirt was hard to button-up. I was so anxious to finish dressing I didn't know what to do.

I glanced often at Mr Chandles and if there was any strain the strain must have been inside him. He looked calm. Even when he walked up and down from his room to the kitchen and back. I had not forgotten the sick-room but the noises there were very quiet. I could hear the footsteps moving softly about.

I went to see myself in the glass now. I looked so different standing there with brown pants and sky-blue shirt. It almost didn't look like me. It was strange and very good.

I didn't stay long in front the glass. I put the clothes I had slept in into the grip and I stopped a little to think if there was anything else at all to go in. Nothing at all. I closed the grip, buckling it up with the belt.

All the time my heart was beating very fast. I went out now into the kitchen to wash my face. It was then I remembered that my tooth-brush was already put into the grip, but it would have to stay there. I would just scrub my teeth with my fingers and wash my face and there would be a towel down in the bathroom to wipe my face with. The different smells in the house were getting very strong. I didn't take any time over washing my face and scrubbing my teeth. When I was running back up the steps from wiping my face in the bathroom Mrs Princet was passing down with a bundle of dirty clothes. The shock of the bad smell sickened me. I wondered how Mrs Princet could hold those clothes in her hand.

I went back into the kitchen again to wait for when Mr Chandles would come out so I could tell him I was ready. I was anxious for him to come back from his room. Out on Celesta Street, although it was so early, everything was lit-up in the sun. There were several people about. There was the smell of early morning, and below me the smell of sweetbroom, and the love-birds had already started coming to our fence. They were not noisy yet. Over the houses it was misty and if you looked towards the cane-lands you could see the mists white and thick and you couldn't see where the coconut tree was.

I watched the people about in Celesta Street. Most of them were going towards the Coffee Street. They walked very quickly. But it was so early the windows of most of the houses were not open yet. You couldn't see the curtains flying about. Perhaps when we left the curtains would be flying about. Perhaps it would be a bright Christmas Eve here on Celesta Street.

I walked into the dining-room, then into the drawing-room so Mr Chandles could hear me and know I was ready. He hadn't been in there long but it was I who was impatient. But it was time to go. I walked back through the dining-room and to the kitchen again. I did not exactly stamp but I was walking so Mr Chandles could hear my footsteps. Back in the kitchen the elderly lady was out and packing little phials in a corner. I didn't know if she upset any but the medicine-smells reeked in the place.

'Hurry up,' she said. 'He's waiting for you.'

'Where he is?'

She pointed to the old lady's room.

'I ready long time,' I said.

'Well call him out. He just sitting down,' she said, and she smiled a little as if there was something about it that amused her.

'What about Mrs Chandles?' I said.

'Oh, she travelling home. She wouldn't last out the day.' She was going back into the room.

132

'Bye-bye,' I said.

'Bye-bye. Safe journey.'

And then it came to me that I was going away without even going in to see Mrs Chandles. It was very bad. This was the last of Mrs Chandles and for me the last of everything in this town. I looked out on Celesta Street again, my heart very excited. I wasn't glad to leave Celesta Street and yet I was glad I was going. The mist was still over the houses. If you didn't look carefully you wouldn't have seen the fine drizzle coming down. It was coming down more like spray. I went in to see Mrs Chandles.

On opening the door I saw Edwin who signalled to me to step back out. I went back into the drawing-room and Edwin came to me.

'I just want to tell you,' he said, 'Things will change up here this morning. As soon as the old lady pass out Linden has to go. No wedding here – no nothing. I think it right you should know.'

I was shocked. I knew a storm was to break but I did not think it would be so soon. I looked up at him.

'You don't know,' he said, 'this is something going on for ages. Now Mother put the house in my name he'll have to go. I can't put up with him. Too dam' bombastic.'

He was waiting for me to say something, but I didn't know what to say. I was still on his side. He seemed bristling for action.

'You'll take it easy,' I said.

'Edwin always takes it easy. Don't frighten for me. But tell your mother. I don't know if she'll send you back.'

'No,' I said, 'I wasn't planning to come back.'

'I can't look after you,' he said, 'and I don't know where *they'll* be.'

'I'm not coming back, Edwin,' I said.

'You not coming back?'

'No. I'll miss you though.'

'Oh, well, I don't know what to say,' he said. 'But in case you don't come back, shake flesh. You is a gentleman.' He stretched out his hand to me and I put mine in his and we shook and he said, 'Till we meet again.'

I answered, 'Till we meet again.'

I was feeling overcome. I left him quickly and went in to see Mrs Chandles.

The rains drizzled a little heavier as Mr Chandles and I walked up Romaine Street. The school-yard was deserted, as I looked back, but a few of the houses around had their doors half-open. I passed Owen's house but Owen's doors were not half-open. I had not seen Owen for many days.

Mr Chandles walked beside me and so tall and big he was that his shadow stretched out like a lamp-post. My shadow was tall, too, but tiny beside his. You could see the sun getting up, glinting on the panes of the windows. You could tell the Dry Season was here because the sun was not usually so bright so early in the morning. I watched this and I watched the rains drizzling down and I thought, here was the Devil and his Wife again, fighting on Christmas Eve. But the drizzle had slackened quite a bit now. We were hardly getting wet and the wind was blowing the fine spray into our faces. My shoes creaked a little and I tried to walk straight, and I was feeling very strange in these new clothes.

Every now and again cars swished by on the Coffee Street before us. We could see the people, crowds of them, walking along the pavements. I couldn't get Mrs Chandles out of my mind. Perhaps it would have been better if I had not gone into that room. In my mind I kept seeing what was stretched out there on the bed. That was what Mrs Chandles looked like. Although she wasn't dead yet. They had already swept the room and arranged it so people could come in to see the dead. There was a white cloth bandaging her chin and tied in a bow at the top of her head. That was done so she wouldn't die with her mouth open. Then they wouldn't have to break it shut. But she was still gasping breathlessly.

I had not stayed long in the room. I just looked at what was on the bed. The room had been clean and tidy and sweet with the smell of lavender water. I had told Mrs Princet good-bye and I had watched Mrs Chandles and had said good-bye just for the sake of saying it. The elderly lady had come in then and she had said, 'Shake Mrs Chandles' hand, you wouldn't see her again.' I had hesitated, and Mrs Princet had said, 'Go on, shake it, shake hands,' and I had gone up to the bed and held Mrs Chandles' hand. It felt just like any other hand. Only bony and small and very hot. Mr Chandles had stood up already, and I, too, was anxious to go. I had said good-bye again and Mrs Princet had said to me, don't forget to look her up when I got back.

On the High Street the big stores were just opening. They were opening earlier than usual for the Christmas Eve. The crowds were already quite thick and I thought to myself what would it be like in the market this morning! If I knew the market at all I knew what it would be like. Christ! I thought.

Thinking of the market I remembered Brinetta and I was glad for remembering her now. For she had slipped entirely from my mind. I thought, Look how Brinetta had gone away forever, and how I was leaving for good now and she wouldn't know, and she might never know Mrs Chandles died this year.

The grip was hard to carry and Mr Chandles helped me with it part of the way. When we got down to the wharf there seemed to be hundreds of travellers about and some were sitting down on their grips under the trees where the big bus stand was, and many were getting on to buses, and there were buses rolling off and there were some that had just arrived on the wharf and crowds seemed to be streaming from those all the time.

If ever there was a mêlée this was one. You could hear the talking and laughter plainly as it came from the lighters near the fish market. There was a commotion in the seamen's hostel and people were standing outside and looking up. I wondered if Mr Chandles was disgusted and I looked at his face but his head was turned up to the veranda of the seamen's hostel. My heart was excited beyond the telling. I looked up and down the railway line but there was no sign of any trains. The sea was very quiet. You couldn't even see the blue of it. It was silvery and lifeless in the sun.

We reached the bus stand and I rested the grip down and the next bus for Princes Town hadn't lined up yet. When they lined up that was the time you could get on. We stood up under the trees and the place still smelled freshly of early morning and I seemed in a strange way to be taking in the whole feeling of the town. Things seemed pressing in upon me. My heart was full to bursting.

Mr Chandles began talking of the regatta and he pointed out Farellon to me. Farellon must have been so tiny and the sea was so dazzling that I could not see what he was pointing out. But I made out I saw it. I looked round at the waterfront and at where the railway station was and I knew the lumber place was at the back of me, right at the back behind the hostels. I knew this and other things too. But the town was still very strange. I had spent a year here and I was standing on the wharf now and I was a stranger in the big place.

An Indian woman, one of the hordes of vendors, came by with a tray on her head, and was crying out 'Groundnuts! Channa! Crack

135

and converse!' This made us laugh. Although I had my own money, Mr Chandles called for two packets of each. He kept one for himself and gave me the other. I didn't know why I was so cheered to see him cracking groundnuts and eating and conversing with me. But I didn't want to eat yet so I put mine into my pocket. I was rather surprised to see him taking refreshments in the street!

The bus lining up jerked me from my thoughts. Mr Chandles let me go in and then he handed me the grip. I was going with it to my seat but the conductor showed me the place where such things were put (I had forgotten) and he put it there for me and I went and sat in a seat by a window where Mr Chandles was just outside. He stood there talking to me. He reminded me where to catch the Rio Claro bus when I got to Princes Town. He said that at Rio Claro there would be no trouble getting the Mayaro bus. Jump into any red bus, he said.

And then the engine of the bus started up again and Mr Chandles took my hand. 'Cheerio,' he said. 'We'll look out for you the day after New Year's. Say hello for me. Okay – okay then!'

I said 'Okay then' to him, too. It was strange saying 'okay then' to him. As the bus swung away and made the big curve I saw him standing there and I kept looking back to watch him. And then I turned in front again and watched the bus speed beside the All Nations Seamen's Hostel, then up Chacon Street, and it seemed as if it was going to pass at the foot of the Naparaima mountain. Everywhere we passed the town was alive with people. We passed places I had never seen before and big stores I had never even heard of. The bus went up a long incline. I looked out of the window and all the people and side streets and shops with beautiful Christmas decorations were falling back.

Mount Naparaima was on the other side and I did not get up to go and see how near it was. I was thinking of what time I would get to Princes Town, and I knew how long it should take from there to Rio Claro. When I got to Rio Claro I would be all right because all the red buses went to Mayaro. Before evening time I would be with Ma and Sil and Felix and Anna. My thoughts were racing.

This bus was a fast one. The Mayaro bus was not so fast. I wondered if it would be Edgill and Balgobin again. If it was Balgobin again you wouldn't have to tell me how surprised he'd be to see me. I wondered if he would give that scandalous laugh again. That laugh annoyed people but I liked to hear it. I would laugh too because I would be so glad to ride the Mayaro road again.

The bus was pulling out of the town now. The red-roofed houses were falling back and now the places were getting different and there were no pavements here but only grass on the sides of the road. It was strange because I could not remember these places at all. I wondered where would the cane-lands be from here? I wondered where would you see the cane-fires if you stood here in the night and the crop-time was on? You could hardly notice it was drizzling again. Here the place was really different and the houses were not one beside the other now but in places very widely apart. They were older and unpainted and there were no fences around them and they looked free in the big spaces. I could not remember these parts at all.

I closed the window because the rains were almost pouring down now. I sat down cosily and there was a lot of talking inside the bus. It was cosy to sit with the windows closed and the rains pouring and the bus speeding along the wet road. The talking was very cheerful. I remembered the mountain and suddenly I looked back but all the windows were closed because of the rains. The bus roared on and my mind went on Mrs Chandles, who was dying, and Mr Chandles – so strange of late, and now homeless; and I thought also of Mrs Princet, and I thought of Edwin and that dollar – I thought of all the mixed-up things, of all the funny things, in fact, which made the year at Romaine Street.

Other titles by Michael Anthony
in the Caribbean Writers Series

Green Days by the River
Introduction by Gareth Griffiths
A perceptive novel about a boy on the edge of adult responsibilities. It is the story of Shellie, a Trinidadian boy who moves to a new village and there meets two girls. He is charmed by Rosalie but he is attracted to the more cheerful and accessible Joan.

1973   208pp   435 98030 0   CWS 9

Cricket in the Road and Other Stories
Introduction by the author
These stories are told with the freshness and directness one has come to expect of Michael Anthony. They are all set in Trinidad and one of them 'Enchanted Alley' was the crystallizing of an idea that led him to write *The Year in San Fernando*.

1973   128pp   435 98032 7   CWS 16

The Games Were Coming
Introduction by Kenneth Ramchand
Leon is in training for the great bicycle race in the Southern Games in Trinidad. He is so obsessed by the race that he has dismissed everybody in his life, even his girlfriend Sylvia. But she makes sure it doesn't stop there.

1977   128pp   435 98033 5   CWS 17

All That Glitters
Beautiful Romeen returns home to Trinidad from Panama bringing a trunk full of presents – but who has stolen the glittering gold chain? There is much to delight in and much that lingers in the memory.'
h Book News

1983   224pp   435 98034 3   CWS 25

idea I was there. People are—are very sorry for me and poor little Jim."

Alfred moved his hand.

" Can't you hear, Father? I daren't speak much louder. There's a man only three beds away."

" Can hear. Sorry for you and Jim—Robert—give them— my love."

" Of course. The book is in a safe place. Much better than the dug-out, I think. It's with Joseph Black."

Alfred's one eye looked worried.

" Christian—gave us away."

" I expect so. But that was accidental. Joseph knows the book is something precious to you and to me. But he can't read it. And there are just two kinds of people who are free from search. The Knights and the Christians. We ought to have had it with Joseph all along. If I hadn't been such a *fool*—oh, well. But, anyway, Father, that's the place for it. The Germans despise the Christians so much that they won't sully their noble hands with turning over their bits of belongings. I asked Joseph if the Germans ever searched their huts, ever had been known to, and he looked at me as if I were mad. Then he said, in his sly way, not his religious way, ' The Lord protects us from search of any kind. Do you search hedgehogs? And if you did, what would you find but lice? ' So you *must* understand," Fred whispered very earnestly, " that the book's safe as long as there are Christians in the land. It's the very place for the Truth. *They* can't understand it, and yet no one else would dream of looking for it among them. And I shall train the men who are to spread it when the time comes. It'll be difficult, but I shall be able to do it."

" Write your name—under mine. And be—less stupid and less—violent."

" Yes, Father."

" Edith," whispered Alfred.

" Who's that? "

" My baby girl."

" But what do you want me to do about her? " Fred was almost convinced his father was wandering, and yet his one eye looked still intelligent.

" Don't know. Nothing—to be—done. Must be left.

In time——" Alfred's whisper died away. He shut his eye.
The pain was dull now. He opened his eye again and was
quite sure that the old Knight von Hess was sitting there
instead of Fred. The Knight did not speak; his fine hooked
nose was bent kindly down on Alfred; his eyes looked pleased.
Alfred tried to greet him, but it was too much trouble and after
all it was Fred sitting there. So that was all right. He
drifted off into unconsciousness. No one disturbed them.
For hours Fred sat there till his father's hand began to get
cold.

THE END